Remembering Your Soul Purpose

A Part Of Ascension

Second Edition

Karen Bishop

Remembering Your Soul Purpose
A Part Of Ascension
Second Edition

ISBN-10 1-60145-013-3
ISBN-13 978-1-60145-013-5

Printed in the United States of America.

Booklocker.com, Inc.
2005

Cover art by Julie Sartain
Author photo by Ross Stubbings

~*Dedication*~

This book is dedicated to my mother, who beautifully embodies the loving energy of the Mother.

Contents

Introduction .... *vii*

Foreword ....*ix*

Remembering Your Path ....*xv*

Module 1: Why Is Remembering Your Soul Purpose A Part Of
    Ascension? *1*

Module 2: Using Your Soul Purpose To Create The New World *9*

Module 3: A View Of The New World Soon To Come *13*

Module 4: Your Destined Reality *17*

Module 5: Your Last Incarnation To Your Rebirth *39*

Module 6: Your Special Gift *65*

Module 7: Your Geographical Home On Earth.....................*87*

Module 8: Your Bloodlines *119*

Module 9: Your One Hat *137*

Module 10: Your Numerology.................................*159*

Module 11: Your Road To Heaven...........................*169*

Module 12: Your Way To Success *199*

Module 13: Your Own Special Team.......................... *203*

Module 14: Your Soul Purpose: Putting It All Together *211*

To Sum Things Up...*235*

Appendix A: Numerology Number Meanings *237*

About the Author *283*

Introduction

WELCOME TO *Remembering Your Soul Purpose/A Part of Ascension*.

The purpose, desire and passion of this book is to activate within you what you already know. If the information presented here feels familiar and comfortable for you, it is simply because you already knew it. And as always, if anything does not feel quite "right" for you, just throw it right out of your consciousness and let it go.

There is no right or wrong, good or bad, or any precise way to get to "Heaven." No one knows more than another what really "is," as all is just an illusion. As we are continually making everything up (including this grand Shift Of The Ages!), we need only embrace the concepts and realities that feel good and right for each of us. It is usually best to make up our own reality anyway, as that is precisely what we are in form to do! And with all the answers already within you, this book will only serve to excavate them.

If you find yourself becoming tired or in a fog while reading any of this material, it is only because you are stretching and expanding your mind to higher levels. If this happens, just take a break and come back to it at a later time.

Know that all of the information presented to you in this book comes from my personal experiences and travels in the higher realms, from my own ascension process and from a deep connection to myself at a higher soul level. This information does not come from any written materials of others or from any channeled information from higher beings.

Remembering Your Soul Purpose: A Part Of Ascension is presented to you in fourteen modules or segments. Twelve of these modules are interactive, while two are articles for you to enjoy which depict and represent the general picture of our New reality. After each of the twelve interactive modules, you will be asked to participate through *Your Remembering Journal*. Your journal is for you to keep and refer to whenever you choose. At the conclusion of the book is a section where you can "put it all together," giving you an opportunity to view a snapshot of who you really are and why you are here on this planet Earth at this current time.

May your experience with this book bring you Heaven in your heart, starlight in your soul and miracles in your life in these miraculous times!

Welcome aboard and God bless,
Karen

Foreword

IN THE SUMMER OF 2001, I was involved in a very minor auto accident. No injuries were incurred, except for mine, which would become the beginning of my ascension process. At that time I had no idea what was actually involved in ascension...only a general knowledge deep within me that something monumental would eventually be happening on the planet...and I knew that that was precisely why I was here.

This minor auto accident created a crushed right leg for me in the form of a severe tibia fracture. But the other ramifications of the accident were far more significant. While waiting the four days for surgery, I had never been more calm. Even while lying on the gurney just prior to receiving anesthesia, my big, beautiful and loving non-physical guide was there assisting in choreographing every detail to my best advantage. At that time, I was also told by non-physical beings that when I awoke, I would not be the same. I could see a higher part of myself in meetings in the higher realms with my soul group...planning something of a very timely nature. Something monumental was about to occur.

"Fine," I thought. "No problem. Everything looks to be in perfect order." And this, as I continually came to know, is the way of ascension. All is always in divine perfect order even though it appears otherwise. And when I awoke, it appeared otherwise. There seemed to be nothing left of me but the souls of my shoes. The "false" parts of my personality, the parts of me that I had developed in this lifetime in order to survive, the lower and more densely vibrating ego parts of me were totally gone, seemingly washed away in some strange and dramatic internal tsunami.

In this state, I have to say, I felt overwhelmingly vulnerable. This vulnerability, along with a lack of oxygen to my brain because of severe blood loss, created a state of panic and anxiety within me. Who in the world was I now? Where had my identity gone? And where, oh where, was my power? I had not had a bath, washed my hair, brushed my teeth, or been out of bed for eight days when a few friends came to visit. As they both arrived independently, they each remarked that I had never looked so beautiful. I thought that they were being overly polite, but both denied that this was the case. It became evident later on that what they were observing was the original innocence. And with much of my ego self washed away and removed, what was left was a much more pure and direct connection to Source. And this more pure and direct connection to Source *was* my power, only I had not been in this way of being ever before in this lifetime.

In one intense, immediate and dramatic experience, I had undergone a massive healing, enlightening and purification process to get me to where I needed to be at that particular time. Before we were born, we chose the roles that would most perfectly suit us in order to assist with this one of-a-kind Shift Of The Ages taking place on our beautiful blue planet Earth. When the vibration of the planet reaches a certain frequency, we are then activated to begin our roles that we intended at soul levels before birth (or rather before we infused our soul energies into these particular physical bodies). This time is different for everyone and dependent upon your role being activated within you at precisely the time it is needed.

In my case, I had agreed to "go first." It has been my experience in many, many life forms to carry the energy of "beginning." And even in this current life experience, I continually find myself in situations where I go first and set up and pave the way for all others to follow. So immediately prior to September 11, 2001, I needed to be ready to fulfill my role and to fulfill my soul purpose for my particular contribution to this creation of the Shift Of The Ages. September 11 created one of the first big ripples in the pond that would begin the much more rapid stirrings of ascension, and I needed to be on board.

For me, I was nowhere near ready. And this is why I experienced such a rapid and intense "crash course" of the ascension process. Even though I had been an avid reader of spiritual and metaphysical material for many years, been born wide open and psychic with the ability to travel through different dimensions, and continually been in a life of service while going through several healings, I would soon find that the ascension process would create within me and take me to places I could never possibly have gone otherwise. The ascension process continued on for me. Within this process I experienced strange and baffling symptoms and realities that certainly made me wonder if I was going insane or really losing it. And with a leg that prohibited me from going anywhere for a few years, I was forced to stay put, become grounded, and move *through* and embody all these many changes and shifts within me. I also had two more big leaps that were once again intense and rapid, but these left me in a place of living in the higher realms (or higher dimensions) and enabled me to report back to others who were at different phases of their ascension journeys.

The beauty of the ascension process is that we evolve through complete and direct experience...not from teachings and writings of others...and in this amazing and perfect space, we come to really know what it is like to live, create, love and exist in a much higher vibrating way. And in very many instances, things were not what we had been taught or told. It is much more simple, loving, non-judgmental, beautiful and truly amazing than that.

Yes, the ascension process places us in a space of truly *being* a higher vibrating human as we continue on with this process of becoming human angels of light. No more talking of spiritual matters...ascension creates a more evolved human who is now *being* the higher ways.

This book then, is originally intended for lightworkers. Because lightworkers as a whole have agreed to pave the way for all others and to go first. In my case, I needed to pave the way for other lightworkers. This book then, is for you. So if any of the references, concepts or terminologies seems confusing, it is only because they are based on the assumption that you have already come to know what they mean. This is also basically the second book from me. It was written and is coming out first because it explains and relates to where many lightworkers currently are on their journeys to Heaven. A much more basic, detailed and preliminary ascension book (or manual) will be written second for those coming later on through the stepping stone world. *Remembering Your Soul Purpose/A Part Of Ascension* was needed *now* and created for the first two waves of lightworkers.

And where are most of these lightworkers now in regard to their journeys? As this book goes to print in January of 2006, we have reached critical mass in the Shift Of The Ages. It was reached in August of 2005. Our mission was successful. There is much elation in the higher realms. We did it! This means that many lightworkers are now poised and ready to begin creating the New World. Yes, we are now ready to *finally* create a world of the higher ways...a world of our dreams...a world that we have always envisioned and known could be possible.

Who are you? What will your contribution be? Will you remember what you came to do, to be and to create? It is my strongest and deepest desire that this book will activate within you who you are and what you know at the highest levels of your being. Here in lies my deepest and most magical wish for this book.

"The future belongs
to those who believe
in the beauty of their dreams."

Eleanor Roosevelt

•••

Remembering Your Path

March 1998

WHO AM I? WHY AM I HERE? What is my purpose and path? What is my contribution? Have you ever asked yourself these questions? All of us, at one time or another, question whether we are in "alignment" with our true selves, whether through a career, our lifestyle and self-expression, or just within each moment.

Before we are born, we choose a path and certain gifts, talents, and personality traits to enable us to achieve our predetermined "mission." But unfortunately, we are born with complete "memory loss." We go along in our lives, feeling that somehow something is missing; that there is something that we are here to do and we just haven't grasped it. Or, we may not feel that we can be our natural, true selves in the current situations in our lives.

When we are in alignment with who we really are and were meant to be, things just seem to "click." Miracles occur. Life seems to flow for us effortlessly. We wake up each morning, joyful to be alive. And while just *being* ourselves, we are sharing our beautiful, special and unique gifts and talents, making this planet a better place to be.

What are your dreams? What are your innermost longings? What would your ideal life look like? Our dreams nag at us because we are *supposed* to fulfill them. And when we live our dreams, which are our subconscious messages of who we are and what we came to do (they are the calling of our destiny), we are creating and contributing to the balance and harmony of the planet. We are being peace. We are being love. We are compassion and acceptance. We are in alignment with our original intentions before birth. And as we give this gift of ourselves to ourselves, we also give it to the whole of the planet.

Living our path and our dreams is having a love affair with our life. It's living out the reason we were put here on Earth this moment in history. When we are on our path, we feel fulfilled. We love what we do, and know we make a difference. Our lives have meaning and direction. Living your path is a natural expression of who you are; an individual role that is beneficial to all life; a calling that exists only for you, and that only you can fulfill. Once you find your path and live it, your life will never be the same. You will be living your life and not just existing. You will be in alignment with Source. You were born to greatness......know that the world has need of you.

"What lies before us and what lies
behind us are small matters
compared to what lies within us.
And when we bring what is within out into the world,
miracles happen."

Henry David Thoreau

•••

Module 1

•••

Why Is Remembering Your Soul Purpose A Part Of Ascension?

"I discovered that people are not
really afraid of dying; they're afraid
of not ever having lived, not ever
having deeply considered their life's
higher purpose, and not ever having
stepped into that purpose and
at least tried to make a difference in this world."

Joseph Jaworski

• • •

THE ASCENSION PROCESS has most certainly begun in earnest on planet Earth, and every living inhabitant who chooses to stay on board will go through this amazing and rare experience. *Very* generally speaking (*The Ascension Primer* book has more detailed information along with a list of symptoms), the ascension process has several phases or steps:

What Is Ascension Anyway?

- We on Earth chose to experience this Shift Of The Ages (a mass rising of consciousness on planet Earth and arrival into a higher dimension), and therefore we knew somewhere in our consciousness that we were here for an unprecedented and monumental event.
- As we made our plans before we infused our energy into human form, some agreed to go first and therefore guide and pave the way for others to follow (these are the first wavers and the lightworkers). This process began for them first, but as the ascension process bumps up exponentially, many are very rapidly experiencing the ascension process now.
- The year 2000 brought in the beginning of the most intense phases of ascension, as we are dying while we are alive. Very generally speaking they involve:

  - A purging and cleansing from within us of darker/denser energies that no longer match the New vibratory rate we are finding ourselves in.
  - A rising of frequency within and without, resulting in New ways of being and a deeper connection to Source and the other dimensions.
  - A magnification of everything that is within us, including beliefs and misperceptions, which will nullify through the purging process.
  - A great growth, intensity and desire to expand and be in our creativity.
  - A step-by-step loss of who we thought we were or our ego; a blown identity.

- Beginning stages of accessing other dimensions through sound, strange visions, foggy thinking short term memory loss, spinning and vertigo, and a variety of other experiences.
- A loss of all attachments, including relationships, careers, and living situations.
- An inability to "do" anything as we are evolving into the way of "being."
- Being in the moment with no agendas or intentional planning.
- Various physical maladies, aches and pains.

- We decided as a group of souls to "begin again" and start over. Therefore, we came together from every part of the universe with representation from every star system and infused our energy into human form for this unprecedented event.
- By having all this representation here on Earth for this Shift Of The Ages, we are then able to bring back this experience of returning to Source through ourselves and then reverberate it to everything back "home," there-by capturing all of the universe.
- We had to "spin off" all the other multidimensional aspects of ourselves where we had infused our energy since the beginning spark of our soul creation, thus refining us to a more pure Source energy.
- We are also "spinning off" from our star parents and star homes as well as all incarnations (which are all occurring at once as time is not linear). Remember, no attachments.
- During this time, the Earth is being restored to its original blueprint where it will again be a playground for creation.
- This time, we will take creation further than the energies of Lemuria or Atlantis and be able to create freely a very New planet Earth of our making and desires.
- As we continue with the ascension process of returning to Source, we will be vibrating higher and higher, and some will eventually become the New stewards or angels for the New planet Earth and beyond, while others will depart to higher vibrating universes and start anew.
- All the current angels, galactics, non-physical beings of light

and every other existing entity in this universe will follow our path and ascend after we do. We are showing the way for all else to benefit from and follow. Yes, we are starting over.

- As all creation is orderly with specific hierarchies, some will complete their "missions" here after the New universe and New Earth are established and move on into a brand New hierarchy of a much higher vibrating and different universe (another of endless universes) and begin again at the "bottom rung."
- Because these souls are leaving and completing their experiences in the current universe as they have done it all and gone as far as they can go here, they have chosen to leave an incredible New palette behind through their creations of a New and clean structure for all who follow to utilize and experience after they are gone.
- So then, some will stay and become angels and guiding beings of light and others will move on to a New and higher universe.
- The planet Earth is the template and blue jewel where it is all happening for the Shift Of The Ages.

So What About Soul Purpose?

As the ascension process involves the spinning off and cleansing of all that has been created before and all that is not of a higher vibrational light, something must remain. Because we release and lose so much of who we thought we were and what we thought was real, along with our past creations of self, there is then much more "room" for us to embody more higher vibrational light within us.

And as we begin to live in these higher realms, we begin to remember who we really are as well. The veil is becoming thinner and thinner and much is being revealed. When we begin the final stages of this first phase of ascension, it is as if the masks are removed and we begin to be able to see our beautiful and loving families from the stars in the physical. "I remember you!" will become a common phrase for us as we re-unite as a soul group once again.

When this phase occurred for me, I cried tears of joy as I could finally *see* my beloved soul family and remembered so clearly who we were and what we came to do. There was no foggy guessing or vague familiarity.

The quirks, behaviors and "issues" no longer were visible as all I could see was a higher version of who they *really* were. The blockages were cleared away to reveal my family and others in full living color. What a joy of unity I cannot describe.

It is the same when we transition through the physical death process in 3D. We are re-united with our loved ones in the non-physical and can now see how things unfolded beautifully and what everything really meant at the higher levels. Yes, the ascension process puts us in the higher dimensions, but this time, we are still "alive" and in a physical body.

Even though we are all very connected and made up of the same energy, we are also very different and unique. If we were all the same pure energy of Source, we would become very bored. It is the same scenario that occurred from the beginning. Source got bored, split off from itself, began creating for something to do, and expanded from that.

So then, we have a soul blueprint that carries us wherever we go. We each vibrate in a unique and distinct way that separates us from the whole, but also allows for our contribution to the whole to make it complete.

When we encounter one another in the higher realms, we appear as a "blob" of vibrating colors and energy, but are very easily recognizable by our unique vibrations. It is easy to tell who you have encountered by the distinct combinations of their own unique vibrations and colors and how they "feel" to us.

Have you ever been able to recognize someone by the vibrations and tones in their voice even though you can't see them? Have you ever felt someone standing behind you and instinctively known who they were by how they "felt?" Have you ever felt oh so at home when you connected with someone just by the tones and vibrations that their voice carried?

With the next phase of the New World occurring very readily now beginning in May and June of 2005, many will now be called to finally bring forth their teaching. The conditions had to be right and met and the vibrations had to be perfect to support this time. You cannot take a cake out of the oven until it is ready and done. The vibrations outside of us need to match the vibrations inside of us. Enough of the population needed to turn from the old, summon something different and be willing to embrace and allow the New. Things needed to get very uncomfortable for this to occur and this is precisely what created the shift of critical mass in August of 2005. In addition, the inner vibrations of many were now much higher and the outside world was simply not reflecting the higher ways that were embodied within. And now with the conditions ripe for many to come forth embodying the ways of the higher realms, they will most predominantly do it through their vibrations. When teaching, we are now at a point where we are totally embodying what we came to express, and thus, vibrating it. Our presence alone will shift the energy around us as we enter a space.

Our individual vibrations remind me of a graph of different tones and ups and downs. If we were to look at our blueprints in this way, we would also see almost exact graphs for those of twin souls or group souls (as they are the same) that split off from Source as one and then split off from their singular original split.

Their energies go up and down in the very same rhythms and flows and at the same times. It is very similar to partners ice dancing almost as one. There is a flow and rhythm that is identical and therefore, very easy to blend together in blissful comfort, unity and what feels like completeness with a very strong familiarity. These twin-like souls are basically *looking at themselves* and when together, feel as though they are in the company of themselves.

But even though these are the closest souls in similar vibration, as their creation occurred during the same moment, there-by when the conditions and surrounding energies were vibrating a particular way along with other components of creation, there are still subtle differences between all souls.

We are all so beautiful in our own unique and special ways. We each have something to offer that is so very vital to the universe. We each have an amazing contribution to make that only we can make in a way like no one else. This universe would not be the same without you in it. Your presence here affects all of the whole. You are so vitally needed.

Module 2

●●●

---

*Using Your Soul Purpose
To Create The New World*

AS WE COMPLETE the first phase of the ascension process, we find ourselves cleansed and purified with a brand new identity we had not experienced in the old world. Although this can create a bit of an identity crisis, what remains is the purer "gold nugget" of our higher selves. We are literally being reborn and reincarnated, only this time we remained in physical bodies!

Yes, much that did not vibrate in these New and higher ways has been removed within us. The illusions we held of who we thought we were (or who others were!), with much of our egos intact, are no longer there. Although it certainly created a challenge having a loss of identity and not knowing who in the world we were looking at in the mirror, the end result places us in a position of finally finding out who we *really* are.

The ascension process has put us in a New state of being as well. Finding it more and more difficult to "do" anything and rapidly losing our desire to make anything happen is a natural process of evolution into a higher being of light. This New higher being only knows how to "be." Creating now occurs by using our intent (which is the masculine) while we allow (which is the feminine) our desires and supports for our creations to come *TO* us.

And as we have lost so much of our ego identities and our desires and abilities to make things happen from our old mental patterns of doing it all ourselves and through our "ego" ideas, we are embodying so much more of a connection to Source and to who we *really* are. The ascension process has greatly assisted in getting us out of the way to allow for our higher version of us, or our soul, to emerge as our new and original identity.

Not feeling like doing anything, having no passion, an inability to access words or thoughts, and feelings of powerlessness are simply symptoms of getting the "old" versions of ourselves out of the way so that our bright, shining and clear souls can emerge. When we can begin experiencing the connection and embodiment of our soul energy, which is a higher and eventually continuous connection to Source, all flows effortlessly and we are ALWAYS on track!

As things are now beginning to manifest almost instantly in these higher vibrations, and a part of us certainly remembers this way of being, we have also found that we have a very low tolerance for red tape, hoops to jump through, and long processes to achieve any end result. These ways of the old world are soon to become obsolete, as we are now wired for the New human and New World.

Since we have given nearly everything up (a good ascension mantra would be "give it up, give it up, give it up!"), we can find ourselves in an unfamiliar state of a type of boredom, as we are finding it more and more difficult to exist in and be a part of the old world.

A large part of what is left for us then, is our creativity. And with this higher embodiment of the energy of our soul, we will become guided and connected more and more to who we are and what we are perfectly wired for creating.

With a New state of being which involves simply vibrating our own unique vibration while being in the moment with no agendas, no planning and no intentional acts of making things happen, creating the New World involves like energies attracting like energies in perfect synchronicity and timing, all while we are totally enjoying ourselves and having fun creating. And it is glorious when it happens!

This is the way we will be living in the higher realms and the New World.

So then, please join me for a glimpse into the mechanics of our New World and how your special contribution is so vitally needed and treasured. As planned from the beginning, your special place in the New World is just waiting for you to fill!

Module 3

●●●

A View Of The New World Soon To Come

January 2003

IMAGINE BEING VERY aware of who you are. You *ARE* your special gifts and talents. You naturally vibrate them. They are effortless for you. You love who you are and are simply "being." You don't vibrate exactly like anyone else. Your particular energy is unique to you...a perfect compilation of your incredible gifts and talents which result in a "beingness" that only you possess. No one expresses their particular gift in exactly the particular way that you do. You wake up each morning joyful to be alive. You cannot wait to be and do what you came to be and do. You have a passion and joy for where you choose to direct your vibration...for what, how and where you choose to create. The opportunities for expansion and creation are never ending.

You live in a community where all is in harmony and balance. Your particular community has, at its hub, a particular vibration that you resonate with. There are other communities on your beautiful planet and each has its own particular vibration, or theme. Each community is in vibratory resonance with that same unique vibrational identity of the geographical spot on Earth it is located upon. You are very connected with those in your community, as they belong to your soul family. You remember and know each other well. You have a great love, caring and appreciation for your family as you have been together since time began. You are joyful to be in each other's presence. You are known for who you are and how you vibrate, so when your community needs that niche filled, you are naturally the one to fill it. It is expected that you will, as you are highly revered for who you are, and your vibration naturally completes the perfect harmony and balance of your community. You don't need to be "off " and "on," as you are continually "being" and doing your gifts, talents, joy and passion, all effortlessly. You are in perfect alignment with Source energy.

In your community there are gardeners, architects, inventors, artists, chefs, writers, musicians, multidimensional communicators, and more. Your community interacts in perfect harmony with nature, the nature spirits, with the planets, and with all of life. All is represented, needed, appreciated and accepted.

What is not needed does not exist, as there would be no need to create it and it could therefore, not be sustained through thought and experience. Your community utilizes and flows with the energy of the planetary alignments, as they are part of the whole as well. You each have a specific and individual vibration along with the identical vibration of the whole. Everyone and everything has a perfect niche and all is effortless. Your needs are continually met at all times, therefore there is never an experience of using up your energy in a direction that does not support the expression of *YOU*. Source energy flows with no resistance, as you realize that you are yourself, an extension of Source. There is regular communication and visitation with light beings and beings from other dimensions. Higher knowledge is easily accessible and experiencing other worlds is a common occurrence. You are all united in the same goal and in the same direction, with no need for resistance of any kind, creating a continual channel for Source energy. You are all one.

Art and creation abound. Quality hand made works of art fill your home and enhance your environment. You feel good just having them around you. They raise you up. These creations are a contribution of each individual's sharing and expression of who they are, as are yours. Architecture is magnificent. There are water wheels, windmills and unusual ways to harness the ever abundant energy that surrounds you. All structural creations are in perfect harmony and alignment with nature. There is no monetary system, as everything needed is fulfilled by someone expressing and being their gifts and talents, their passion and joy.

All is freely given. To live in your community, you need only to be, to express and to allow. *Being* who you are at the deepest level (from your soul), *expressing* through your creations and *allowing* source energy to pour through you. Do you remember our communities? Do you remember the New World that we came to show, guide and create?

This way of living and being and these New communities is where we are rapidly headed. As all of the old patterns, old lower vibrational ways of thinking, feeling and expressing begin to fall away within us as part of this ascension process, we are quickly accelerating and ascending into higher beings of light that have no choice but to create a world on the outside that is in alignment and matches who we have become on the inside. What will be your own unique contribution to make that is in perfect alignment with Source energy and with *YOU*?

Module 4

•••

Your Destined Reality

"Often people attempt to live their lives backwards.
They try to have more things, or more money,
in order to do more of what they want,
so that they will be happier.
The way it actually works is the reverse.
You must first be who you really are,
then do what you need to do, in order to have what
you want."

Shakti Gawain

•••

AND WHAT YOU really need "to do" is simply vibrate and be more of who you are!

In March of 2004, during the Spring Equinox here in the United States, I experienced a great personal shift into a much higher dimension. Although I had experienced intense, rapid and massive shifting two times before, this one would really stick. For me, it was most certainly a rebirth into a brand new me, and a crossover into the new way of being in a much higher dimensional world. Although it lasted for a few weeks, I was not very comfortable having such an acute awareness and heightened abilities, so I chose to return to the current planetary vibrational status. It was lonely for me out there! There seems to be a pattern we are experiencing regarding our own personal rebirth and transition into the higher realms. For early ascenders, many experienced this personal rebirth around the time of their birthday during the year when they are finally ready to "cross over" into a higher dimension. Mine arrived precisely at that time as well. (A brief note: April and May of 2005 brought in a mass ascension of first and second wavers.)

Through the eyes of this much higher awareness while being in the higher dimensions, as well as during times of dimensional travel, I was able to see with total clarity a higher level of reality. As I viewed my surroundings, many things were quite evident. For one, we were all driving around in automobiles. Knowing we had the ability to go where we needed to go with the power of intent alone, driving seemed very cumbersome.

We only needed to think, feel and embody our new destination and we could be there in an instant, but we had somehow forgotten. It was all *within* us, and we were utilizing objects *outside* of us to accomplish our traveling desires. The same is true for our electronics. We are using *outside* technology and we are now wired for *internal* technology.

While driving through a shopping area, I was baffled by the exchange system we had been living in. It seemed that everyone had bought into a limited idea that there was not enough. We did not believe that we could create infinitely with no limitations. Instead, we were exchanging money for goods and services, and had become slaves to money. We believed that when the money ran out, so did our ability to acquire.

We believed that we had to "give" something in order to "get" something. It was as if our "knowingness" button had been shut off and we were all existing as walking zombies in a trance of forgetfulness! We had forgotten our power and natural state of being as unlimited creators, with everything we could ever need at our disposal.

But the social structure was the most pronounced. There was no unity. Everyone was separate, living in separate houses and separate worlds. And the most alarming aspect was that we all thought that we were totally responsible for ourselves while we struggled along all alone. We had forgotten that we were all one. No one really connected. I remember being at the airport during this time.

While waiting for my daughter's flight to arrive, I observed all the people sitting in the waiting area. No one was connecting to anyone else. There was pronounced isolation and separateness. Some were reading and some were just staring, believing they were separate and totally responsible for themselves alone, without love, help or support. It seemed so very strange Generally speaking, a view of our current 3D world during this experience certainly revealed that at this level, all was really in divine perfect order. With this higher dimensional remembering and knowingness, it was very easy to see that each of us was creating our own individual world and reality. Each person was perfectly entwined with other individuals according to the universal Law of Attraction. The beliefs of each individual became their own particular world and experience, along with others who shared their belief system and agreed to serve as actors in this "play" that we all had made up. These certainly were ideas we have all read and heard about, but *experiencing* them gave them a whole new meaning for me. I now understood them completely. However we vibrated and whatever we believed to be real became just that. Therefore, worlds existed within worlds, realities within realities, while the "collective" reality formed the foundation.

It appeared that we were on this magnificent playground called planet Earth to create, experience and enjoy. All was an outlet for Source energy to move through and experience itself. It was an incredible and exciting experience of being in another dimension viewing the world according to how it currently existed and why.

"People travel to wonder at the height
of mountains, at the huge waves of the sea,
at the long courses of rivers,
at the vast compass of the ocean,
at the circular motion of the stars,
and they pass by themselves without wondering."

St. Augustine

•••

_____

"Each of us is potentially
the difference in the world."

Marilyn Ferguson

•••

A few years ago, I was standing in a friend's living room and suddenly "popped" into another dimension. This time, two things became very apparent while viewing the world "from the outside" and embodying a total connection with my soul. We had been cut off and shut down from our true power as creators because:

1. The vibration of the planet up until then was not high enough to support the kind of instant manifestation and soul connection we were accustomed to, and

2. There had been interference from dark forces for eons, thus resulting in personal issues, blockages in our energy causing health situations, and total interference and control in the physical from these lower, darker frequencies.

It was also evident that emotions were a great gift and in high demand, resulting in great anticipation and joy being experienced by souls as they looked forward to the experience of being in a human body. Even the strong emotions of grief, devastation, pain and suffering were felt and viewed by souls as a wonderful experience. Feeling emotions seemed to be something that was really fun and greatly valued and an integral part of the human experience. Viewed from a soul level, even the unpleasant emotions of pain were just a small blip, easily handled and no big deal after leaving the human body. It seems that we humans tend to be very dramatic, overly sensitive, and incredible whiners and complainers! Souls seem to know that this is just something that they experience, and all is in order. We humans make much too big a deal about being what we think are victims!

As we have finally reached a much higher vibrational level, and are continuing to elevate vibrationally in exponential amounts, our abilities as creators are heightened as never before. And we are also getting to the levels where we are remembering and experiencing much of this as we are beginning to connect with our souls very consciously now. In addition, with much assistance from non-physical beings of light, and through our diligent efforts as physical beings of light, the lower, darker and denser energies that have been allowed to exist here for eons of time are finally coming to an end. We are vibrating beyond them. So then, creating what we want is easier, faster and more fun

23

than ever before!

Because March, April and May of 2005 brought in an incredible opportunity for ascension for many, resulting in critical mass being finally reached, the time is ripe. And with the opening finally available in April 2005 for the unveiling of the original blueprint for planet Earth as a beautiful Mecca and playground for experience and creation, the road has *finally* been cleared for our creations and our passions to unfold like never before.

Please proceed to the first exercise of your **Remembering Journal** on the following pages, where you will begin to access what has been inside of you for a very long time, just waiting for the opportunity to manifest.

"Man's mind, once stretched by a new idea, never regains its original dimension."

Oliver Wendell Holmes

•••

"Hitch your wagon to a star."

—Henry David Thoreau

"Use the light that is in you to
recover your natural clearness of sight."

—Lao-tzu

•••

Your
Remembering Journal

YOUR *Remembering Journal* is the part of this book where you can express who *YOU* really are. It is the place where you will extract and record the pivotal parts of yourself, enabling you to view a more condensed "snapshot" of your soul purpose, passion and destiny. It is the part that is just for *you*.

Several modules of this book have corresponding sections which comprise your *Remembering Journal*. As you follow along with the book, you will find these sections following the majority of the modules.

So sit back, get comfortable and cozy, and as you relax and enjoy yourself, get ready to welcome the exquisite company of an incredible being.........*YOU*!

Your Remembering Journal

●●●

Module 4:
Your Destined Reality

This exercise comes in three sections. For the first section, please read the question below, along with the guidelines that follow, and then formulate your answer:

1. What would you do/create if you knew you could not fail?

As you begin to formulate an answer, go all out with it. Don't limit yourself to what you think would be possible or probable, but really imagine something big, as all is possible, especially now in these New higher vibrations we are in.

Imagine that you are absolutely successful and had no roadblocks or glitches getting there. Imagine being highly successful at what you do, and highly revered. You are known for doing this particular thing, as you do it so well. This thing you do comes so easily and naturally for you, that people are amazed and delighted by your special gift and look to you as the one to do it. You do it like no other...in your own unique way. You are so good at it, that it comes effortlessly for you, much to the amazement of others, as they cannot figure out how you do what you do...and neither can you.

In addition, it may very well be something that you have *always* wanted to do and known that the time would come one day. The time is finally here. The planet is finally ready for your creation or your vision.

Know that this is so. This is what you came to do.

So then, ***what would you do?***

_____

_____

_____

_____

_____

_____

_____

_____

_____

_____

_____

After you are done answering this question, go on to the next question below:

1. a. What is it about (what you chose to do) , that you really love (or want or need)?

What do you really like about it? Why do you really want to do this particular thing? While you are describing this thing that you would do, really imagine that you are doing it now. How are you feeling and *what excites you about it*? Does it feel oh so much like **YOU** and bring you a feeling of great excitement?

_____

_____

_____

_____

_____

_____

_____

_____

_____

_____

_____

_____

_____

_____

You have imagined doing this particular thing because you are *supposed* to be doing it... otherwise, it would not have even entered your realm of thought or imagination. It is your soul speaking to you. It is your destiny.

Now proceed to the next question, along with the guidelines that follow, and record your answer:

2. If money was no concern, and you had all the time and money in the world, what would you do/create?

Imagine that you had a substantial inheritance that would support you indefinitely with a never-ending flow of money at your disposal (better yet, imagine that you could create *without* money!). You have more time to yourself than you could ever need. What would you create? What would you do with yourself?

Again, go for the top and think big knowing that whatever you needed or wanted was at your disposal and could be successfully done or created with complete certainty. Now, please record your answer.

_____

_____

_____

_____

_____

_____

_____

_____

_____

_____

_____

_____

_____

_____

_____

_____

_____

As the first wave and most recently the second wave of lightworkers are being provided with the opportunity for ascension, all will be provided for them. When you reach this point and are **being** and vibrating who you really are, everything you need will come to you effortlessly. All you need do is to "**be**" about what it is you desire and you will naturally attract it to you. If you simply surround yourself with what you love and what you know, and "do" and "be" it joyously, all else will **COME** to you on its own. Your energies need only be spent in the creating aspects of what you love to express (i.e. art, architecture, design, music, etc.). All else will follow on its own.

In addition, it is part of the plan for substantial amounts of funding to come your way for your very special project. Trust that this will be so, as it will be.

And remember that it is not necessary to list a project. If your answer involves doing something for yourself that makes you feel great, then that is wonderful. You may simply want to travel and experience. In the New World as higher beings of light we are *supposed* to be in situations that make us feel good...plain and simple. It doesn't matter what this is as long as it feels good and right to you. We are here to experience and create absolutely anything that we choose.

Our soul purpose involves two aspects. One aspect relates to our relationship and contribution to the whole, or our service to the planet. The other involves our relationship and contribution to ourselves.

Occasionally, both are the same, but most of the time there are two aspects. The latter, in relationship to ourselves is usually something involving our creativity or what we do for ourselves that brings us great joy and contentment... when time seems to fly by and we totally lose ourselves.

Again, ask yourself this second question:

2. a. What is it about (what you created or did), that makes it so exciting and important to you?

_____

_____

_____

_____

_____

_____

_____

_____

_____

_____

_____

_____

_____

_____

_____

3. In regard to your answers for questions 1. and 2., why is it so necessary to have (what you created or did) on this planet or in this society? Why did you want to do it or experience it? How will you or others benefit? What do you value about it?

_____

_____

_____

_____

_____

_____

_____

_____

_____

_____

_____

Now answer the final question for this module:

4. What is your dream or fantasy about your ideal life?

What would your life look like if you could have the life of your dreams? Imagine it day by day from waking up each morning to going to sleep at night. Where would you live? Who would be a part of your life?

What would you be doing or creating? Why would you live where you do? Why did you pick the "lifestyle" you did? What was important for you to have in your life? Why?

_____

_____

_____

_____

_____

_____

_____

_____

_____

_____

_____

_____

You chose this life because you are *supposed* to be living it. It is what you came to be and experience here on this playground for creating called Earth. And with the higher realms that we have recently arrived in, your time is finally here. The new higher vibrations are the trigger that will activate with rapid speed the creations that you desire.

Welcome to the New Planet Earth!

Module 5

●●●

Your Last Incarnation To Your Rebirth

"Our deepest fear is not that we are inadequate.
Our deepest fear is that we are powerful beyond
measure. It is our light, not our darkness, that frightens
us. We ask ourselves, who am I to be brilliant,
gorgeous, talented and fabulous? Actually,
who are you not to be? You are a child of God.
Your playing small doesn't serve the world.
There's nothing enlightened about shrinking so that
other people won't feel insecure around you.
We were born to manifest the glory of God within us.
It's not just in some of us; it's in everyone.
And as we let our own light shine, we unconsciously
give other people permission to do the same.
As we are liberated from our own fear, our presence
automatically liberates others."

Nelson Mandela, president, Republic of South Africa
from his 1994 inaugural speech

•••

THE NEW WORLD arrived here on planet Earth on December 12, 2004 (12:12). On November 11, 2004 (11:11), an opening or stargate occurred that gave us an opportunity to connect to the higher realms. Within this staircase or energetic opening arrived a magnificent blueprint from above for a higher way of living and being in a much higher dimension. After the opportunity and blueprint arrived through this dimensional opening, the next step was the creation of this New World or higher dimension **on** our planet Earth...only this time in the physical.

From December 12, then, until the equinox in March 2005 (here in the United States), there began an intense preparation. If the New Earth was ready to finally be birthed, the palette needed to be prepared and the foundation laid. During this time, a deeper cleansing occurred. Many who had not as yet experienced ascension symptoms began to experience them in earnest. Anything not energetically in alignment with the higher vibrations of a New dimension was affected. The Earth herself began an alignment process as well, with many shifts and reverberations and lots of cleansing through water (tsunamis and tears). In addition, those who had already gone through much of the first phase of ascension went even deeper, although their experiences were much more mild as they had already become aligned in many ways. With this now intense and radical preparation and cleansing process underway, many more were now brought to even higher levels of vibration within themselves. Many in the dark began to awaken and began to shift. The numbers began growing and now, with many more beginning their process and vibrating higher, the momentum was certainly growing. During this time, many, many more were now being "prepared" for their roles in the New World. And all was in perfect order as we are all programmed to begin our ascension process and reach certain levels when the vibration reaches a certain frequency. We will "activate" according to our plan and the universal plan, as all are one. Timing is always key and the time for many was now.

As each of our plans are different, some began their process much sooner than others (the first wavers). Generally speaking, we planned our purpose and roles before we infused our energies into our current human forms. For instance (as mentioned before), I agreed to "go ahead", and this has always been my path and life experience and therefore, when the planet first began to increase in frequency, my ascension process began in earnest, as I needed to be ready for the

41

specific role that I chose involving assisting others "across" and showing the way. And what a process it was! I had a lot of catching up to do. It is the same for all of us, as we will always be right where we need to be because of this divine orchestration.

The impending arrival of this New World gave all of us an opportunity to choose at a soul level whether we would like to stay and become a part of creating it and evolve into higher beings of light, or to leave and continue our evolutionary process in another reality better suited to the needs of our souls. These choices were made in July, 2004 by our souls and some of us were very conscious of this time of choice while many were not. No matter, as all is always in perfect order and divinely orchestrated. On this note, know that earmarks and pivotal points are continually arriving on the planet that give those who have chosen to leave an opportunity for choice as to *when* they will make their departure. These choices are always in perfect alignment with conditions surrounding these souls that will impact family members and situations in a perfect orchestration supporting more expansion and growth and certainly completion. If the time is not yet right for each soul, they can take the next "train" or energetic planetary opportunity when it arrives. It is truly beautiful to see and greatly supports the knowingness that all is always in divine perfect order.

So then, with the advent of this grand opportunity for evolution greatly accelerating during this year of 2005, we are literally being reincarnated again. As the ascension process involves "dying" while we are alive, we are now reincarnating as New and more evolved humans on the New planet Earth after having gone through much of the "death" process. We are having a rebirth on a new planet and as new humans in a higher dimension. As December 2004 brought in the New blueprint from "above," March 2005 brought in the New (or original) blueprint from "below," as Heaven and Earth finally met.

"Fairy Godmother, where were you when I needed you?"

Cinderella

•••

"I feel that something vast and mysterious is at stake, something known only to me, important only to me."

Jean Martine

•••

And then in August of 2005 we reached critical mass. Next arrived another critical pivotal point of November 11, 2005 (11:11), creating yet another stargate or opening to the higher realms. Only this time the stargate or opening to Heaven completely integrated with the Earth and descended upon her and all her inhabitants. The 11:11 opening this time was much more magnified and certainly pivotal because of reaching critical mass. This means that we are now in the higher realms to stay. We are living and being and existing in the higher realms. No more going back and forth or experiencing "a bit" of higher vibrating existence. It is finally here in a wonderful totality.

How then, do our "old" roles and prior gifts and talents that we contributed to the Old World apply to us now?

For the first phase that occurred in the Old World, we came to shake things up, to spread our light, and to raise the consciousness of the planet. "EVERYONE" was here. There was literally representation from enormous amounts of star systems and other "homes" for this unprecedented Shift Of The Ages. For as each of us experienced the shift and evolutionary process within us in human form, we reverberated it back again to our star "homes" as well for all to benefit and evolve. With all this presence here on Earth of so many advanced beings of light all at the same time and from all over the universe, we felt the plan was assured of success.

And now this old "role" and purpose is over. We need no longer apply our special gifts and talents for the purpose of the first phase as it has now finally been completed. With the success of critical mass, many lightworkers felt an eerie sense of being done. Where do we go from here? Where do we now apply our special gifts and talents? Even though the first phase is now complete, these special gifts and talents remain intact as they are always at the highest levels and not affected by all the internal cleansing we have experienced thus far. So then, our gifts and talents are now ready to be used for creating the New World and basically brought up to even higher levels of expression and purpose.

Let's go back now and reactivate and trigger some of these desires, purposes and talents that are so beautifully imbedded within you and now ready to be brought up to even higher levels of purpose.

Your Remembering Journal
●●●

Module 5:
Your Last Incarnation To Your Rebirth

Your Childhood

For this period of your life (*your childhood*) think of these five things:

1. Something that you loved to do.
2. A task or project that you did successfully and enjoyed.
3. Something that really turned you on.
4. What you were engaged in during your happiest moments.
5. Your most creative outlet.

Write down your answers for **1** through **5** on the lines below:

1.

_____

_____

_____

_____

_____

_____

2.

_____

_____

_____

_____

_____

_____

3.

_____

_____

_____

_____

_____

_____

4.

_____

_____

_____

_____

_____

5.

_____

_____

_____

_____

_____

_____

Then ask yourself these questions regarding your answers for **1** through **5** above:

Why did you love it? OR
Why did you want to do this?

Write down that reason, goal or purpose below for each of your answers:

1.

_____

_____

_____

_____

_____

_____

2.

_____

_____

_____

_____

_____

3.

_____

_____

_____

_____

_____

_____

4.

_____

_____

_____

_____

_____

_____

5.

_____

_____

_____

_____

_____

_____

Follow this process for the *"Adolescent"* and *"Adulthood"* sections as well. For the *Adulthood* section, don't forget to ask these five questions for your **CURRENT** situations too.

Your Adolescence

1.

_____

_____

_____

_____

_____

2.

_____

_____

_____

_____

_____

_____

3.

_____

_____

_____

_____

_____

4.

_____

_____

_____

_____

_____

_____

5.

_____

_____

_____

_____

_____

_____

Why did you love it? OR
Why did you want to do this?

Write down that reason, goal or purpose for each of your answers in
1 through **5**:

1.

_____

_____

_____

_____

_____

_____

2.

_____

_____

_____

_____

_____

_____

3.

_____

_____

_____

_____

_____

4.

_____

_____

_____

_____

_____

5.

_____

_____

_____

_____

_____

_____

Your Adulthood (and CURRENT situations)

1.

_____

_____

_____

_____

_____

_____

2.

_____

_____

_____

_____

_____

3.

_____

_____

_____

_____

_____

4.

_____

_____

_____

_____

_____

_____

5.

_____

_____

_____

_____

_____

_____

Why did/do you love it? OR
Why did/do you want to do this?

Write down that reason, goal or purpose for each of your answers in
1 through **5**:

1.

_____

_____

_____

_____

_____

_____

2.

_____

_____

_____

_____

_____

3.

_____

_____

_____

_____

_____

4.

_____

_____

_____

_____

_____

_____

5.

_____

_____

_____

_____

_____

•Record any themes you notice in all of your responses above and also the areas and arenas where you found this happiness and joy.

_____

_____

_____

_____

_____

_____

_____

•Now look over all your answers and pull out the key words.

_____

_____

_____

_____

_____

_____

•See if you can condense these answers and insights into a single sentence or two (*one for service to humanity and one for self-expression*). For example: "*Connecting to others and the universe in a higher way with undivided and focused attention through animals, writing and nature. Sewing practical and unique designs for the purpose of uplifting others through their environment.*"

_____

_____

_____

_____

_____

_____

_____

_____

_____

_____

_____

_____

Later, as things begin coming together, we will bring these gifts and talents to the higher levels of the New World.

Module 6

●●●

Your Special Gift: Part I

---

*Ludwig von Beethoven was not known for
his social grace, as he was deaf and conversation
for him was difficult and humiliating.
When he received word of the death of a friend's son,
he immediately went to the house,
feeling great grief.
As words were not something he utilized well,
he knew not what to say.
But he did notice a piano in a corner of the room.
He sat down and played from his heart and
emotions with all the love and compassion that he
could. When he finished playing, he left.
Later, the friend told others that no one else's visit
had meant so much.*

•••

WE ALL HAVE a special gift inside of us like no one else. *If you had a friend in need what would you offer?*
I remember a time while in the throes of intense ascension symptoms when I needed help, as I certainly was not capable of helping myself. As I offered myself up to receive and allow, having no other choice, the floodgates opened and assistance poured in.

**"Every time you ask for guidance,
you receive it."**

Gary Zukav

•••

- One friend who was gifted at diagnosing came over and did energetic grounding with me and some balancing body work.
- Another friend who loved to connect and network with her surroundings, took me on a walk.
- A beautiful friend I had always referred to as "walking compassion" called me daily with words of great compassion, support and caring.
- My friend Joy Drake who had created those beautiful little angel cards from the 80's, assured me that they really *did* work. (I continually drew the "birth" card and at times the "patience" card, assuring me when I could not, that all was in divine order.)
- Another very talented friend gave me a reading and took me through EFT sessions.
- A soul partner who lived in another state and had a gift for making money supported me financially until I had progressed enough to manifest my own again.
- My mother talked to me several times a day and offered

that incredible energy of the Mother and the feminine, never tiring of this strange and intense process I was going through, even though she did not understand it.

- Another very close friend guided me through ways of staying positive and keeping my vibration high.
- And then there was my granddaughter Amayah. She was perhaps the most amazing of all as we played, had fun, stayed very in the moment, and marveled at all the wonder around us and within us. She brought back to me the *original innocence*, and a very key part of the ascension process.

We offer others what we do oh so naturally and what our gift is to give. We cannot *NOT* vibrate, do or offer this gift. Several years ago, I could not give enough readings to people. Before I began having regular clients, I used to call everyone I knew and ask them if they wanted a reading. Begging was actually more like it! This is why I *love* writing the energy alerts (see www.whatsuponplanetearth.com) as it gives me a regular outlet for my self-expression. For me, I cannot *NOT* connect to the higher realms on a very regular basis. It is who I am. We simply cannot *NOT* do what we are good at and what we are programmed to do. It flows out from us naturally and we are most certainly *always* in it as we *are* it. If we ever take a break from this part of us, we will always come back to it again as it feels like home.

When we have a special gift and talent that is unique to us, we express it very naturally. It is so much a part of us, that we are rarely aware that we are this way or that we vibrate in this unique and special way, as we are very much *in* it at all times. To others on the outside, it seems very clear, but for us, we are most certainly oblivious! When we do something easily and well, it can be difficult to describe or teach to others.

"How do you connect to and travel to the higher dimensions?" someone might ask me. I could never explain it to them, as I have been doing it for as long as I can remember. Ask a professional baseball pitcher or a golfer how they move their bodies and what they do and they most likely could not explain it to you. The actor Marlon Brando, who has been called the best actor of all time, eventually quit acting as he had such an incredible natural talent for it that he felt he was doing nothing extraordinary. He could not understand what everyone marveled about and he eventually began to feel guilt for something he felt he did not deserve.

"You are born with a character; it is given,
a gift, as the old stories say,
from the guardians upon your birth...
Each person enters the world called."

James Hillman

"A musician must make music,
an artist must paint,
a poet must write, if he is to be
ultimately at peace with himself."

Abraham Maslow

•••

If I had a friend in need I would give them a reading and express to them what is actually happening at the higher levels *or* I would come to their home and sew them some designer pillows, new window treatments, upholster a piece of their furniture or create some other fabric art to bring comfort and beauty to their surroundings.

"You cannot sincerely help another
without helping yourself."

Emerson

● ● ●

Your
Remembering Journal
● ● ●

Module 6:
Your Special Gift: Part I

What would you bring to a friend in need? *(What would you immediately and impulsively offer? How do you usually help? What do you usually and easily give?)*

_____

_____

_____

_____

_____

_____

_____

_____

_____

_____

_____

As we cannot see our special gifts and talents because they come so easily for us and we assume others are made up of these same traits, even though they are not, it can greatly help to ask others how they see us.

On the following page is a *Family and Friends Questionnaire.* If you are comfortable doing so, give it to your significant others and those who know you well and ask them to fill it out. Although a very simple process, this questionnaire is perhaps one of the best tools for identifying who you really are and what you are about. We can rarely see ourselves, but others can see us very clearly. *Good luck with it and enjoy!*

FAMILY/FRIENDS QUESTIONNAIRE

1. What do you think are his/her best skills, talents, and qualities?

2. What is the unique style with which this person gives of himself/herself to life? In other words, what do you think is his/her essence?

3. How would you describe his/her personality?

4. What issues/concerns does this person continually speak of?

5. If this person could create any life he/she wanted, what would that life look like?

6. What kind of work do you think this person is best suited for?

7. What would you ask this person for help with?

Module 6

●●●

Your Special Gift: Part II

"There is a vitality, a life force, an energy,
a quickening that is translated
through you into action.
Because there is only one of you in all of time,
this expression is unique.
If you block it, it will never exist through any
other medium and be lost.
The world will not have it. It is not your business to
determine how good it is,
nor how valuable it compares with other expressions.
It is your business to keep it yours clearly and
directly, to keep the channel open."

Martha Graham

•••

IN THE HIGHER REALMS, all only exists if we entertain thoughts of it in our consciousness. If we do not believe something exists, or do not believe in it and make it real, it will simply not exist as we are not giving it any energy. Time is very much in the moment in the higher realms as well. Anything not in our consciousness for that moment is simply gone. And remember, this ties in as well to our very quick manifesting time now.

At times during the ascension process we may not remember who we spoke to or what we did yesterday and even hours before. What happened last week or that morning may seem like it occurred a lifetime before. We are living very much in the moment now, and can literally begin creating fresh within each moment and at the dawn of each new day. What remains consistent for us then is only what we choose to keep in our consciousness on any regular basis. It is what we choose to keep a connection to. As for the whole, we also create realities according to what the majority or collective are believing and buying into and keeping alive.

On this note, then, the same is true for people. What we focus on in them and what we believe they are about and who they are, brings that into our reality and experience. Now more than ever, people will enter our lives who are matching our own vibrations in some ways. In the higher realms, like energy attracts like energy very rapidly and becomes our realities. There are always pieces and themes of common ground between all those that are in our lives. We may seem more of one particular trait when we are with our friend John, and more of another trait when we are with Leslie, and so on.

What does all this mean? It means that we can literally create and mold people to who we believe they are. If we see their highest form, then that is how they will manifest to us when we interact with them. If we see their darkness, then the same. And in these new higher realms, we are seeing more and more of each individual's highest selves. What we focus on becomes real.

Several years ago I began a new contract with a school district working with a severely physically disabled young man in a Junior High school setting. This being had a history of inappropriate and defiant behavior and his identity and power came from acting out and getting into all kinds of trouble. That seemed to be all he was about. My first step involved consulting with staff and the vice principal regarding putting a new identity in place for him. Their usual response to him when interacting and passing him in the hallway was, "Have you been staying out of trouble lately?" or communications to a similar effect. I encouraged them to instead focus on his new achievements as he was just learning to read and write and had begun to write for the school newspaper. This alone worked magic. He began to get a new image of himself and eventually that was who he became, as well as being highly revered and respected for his new talents.

We can now take this phenomenon to even higher levels as we are now in the higher realms. Remember, manifestation time is very rapid now. What we think about and believe can show up in our space in immediate "time." And in addition, with much of our density and the lower vibrational aspects of ourselves having dropped away through the ascension process, we are now glowing brightly more and more as our true divine selves are most certainly rising to the surface. Eventually, our higher selves are all we will see in each other and we are growing closer and closer to this reality every day.

In addition, through arriving in the higher dimensions, we are able to *see* very clearly who our soul brothers and sisters are in the physical. In these higher vibrational realities, it is beautifully different. It is as if the veil has been lifted and we suddenly decided to remove our masks and reveal ourselves to each other.

"I remember you now! Remember what we came to do? How has it been for you?", we may exclaim. And the feeling and remembering of coming home to our closest family and *seeing* who they really are is simply indescribable (and quite emotional!).

"Let my friends say,
'I like me best when I am with you.'"

Anonymous

"The friend who understand you,
creates you."

Romain Rolland

●●●

Your Remembering Journal
•••

Module 6:
Your Special Gift: Part II

What people do you admire the most and why? Please answer this question on the lines below.

You can draw from relatives, friends, historical figures, celebrities, and even your pet friends. List as many as you feel guided to, but at least four. What is it in these beings that you admire so much?

1.

_____

_____

_____

_____

_____

2.

_____

_____

_____

_____

3.

_____

_____

_____

_____

_____

4.

_____

_____

_____

_____

5.

_____

_____

_____

_____

6.

_____

_____

_____

_____

_____

7.

_____

_____

_____

_____

_____

The reason that you admire these traits in others is because you have them in yourself. We cannot see in another what we do not have in ourselves. And when we *really* see these traits, as they stand out so brightly for us, it is precisely because we are seeing ourselves.

As you list these traits in your journal, know that this is who you *really* are. If you do not believe you are these things, simply ask your closest friends and family. You may also be using these traits in a different arena and in a different way than those you admire. These traits may even be in "temporary hibernation."

And know that if you are not vibrating them fully now, they are most certainly indicating your potential.

After you have described and listed the traits that you admire in others, narrow them down to a few words and write them here to keep for future reference.

_____

_____

_____

_____

_____

_____

This is your potential and the **you** that you came to be!

"Within every desire is the mechanics of its fulfillment."

Deepak Chopra

"If we are *not* capable of doing or having something, we will *not* have an authentic yearning for it."

Debbie Ford

•••

Module 7

●●●

Your Geographical Home On Earth

ALL GEOGRAPHICAL AREAS on planet Earth hold their own special energies and vibrations. Just as each person vibrates in a unique and special way, so do different places on the planet.

Before the New Earth and next phase or New Beginning arrived in December, 2004, there were certain areas on the planet that carried vibrations and portals to the higher realms. These areas naturally vibrated higher and many felt compelled to visit these areas or to live in them.

These higher vibrating geographical areas felt much more like Home, and therefore, lightworkers and beings that vibrated higher were certainly more comfortable there.

These geographical areas served two specific purposes in the Old World (which are actually the same purpose, as all energies are ultimately one). As each area had its own specific vibration or purpose, when one resided or visited there, this purpose and vibration was then activated within them, creating the balance needed for each individual's growth in a very natural way through a sort of "osmosis" or integration by being in the presence of the energies.

For instance, Asheville, North Carolina, in the United States carries the vibration of expression and creativity.

Being a "3" in numerology, it is an amazing place where the arts and any form of self-expression just explode.

With the energy of the feminine deeply intact, it also vibrates loving support, allowing, non-judgment and community and has been described by many as the "mother's womb" or the "New Age Capital of the World."

Creativity is most certainly the main theme, and it serves its purpose well. So then, if one were to reside there for a time, one would begin to express and tap into their creative side, express more of their feminine side, and embody more of the attributes of this area quite naturally by just being there.

As a general rule of thumb for energy is that it only exists for us when it is focused upon or activated, visiting or residing in certain areas then, will activate that particular energy or theme that is within us. Like energy always attracts like or corresponding energy.

In the Old World, we were drawn to and found ourselves in areas that supported our growth and experience by naturally balancing our energies. In addition, we were also drawn to areas to assist in balancing its energies through our own energies as well...all Source energy in this regard was one. We became balanced and activated and the geographical areas became balanced and activated.

When the Shift Of The Ages really began to occur with rapid and intense purpose around 2000, lightworkers were called to specific areas. The purpose was clear and defined with no room for error. We were called to certain areas in numbers for the specific task of building the energies there, there-by creating a dominance of light by condensing as much light as possible into certain areas.

We were certainly in on this plan, whether conscious of it or not, as many found themselves arriving at the hub of certain higher vibrating areas, for reasons unique to each, even though there existed a singular reason at the highest soul levels.

April of 2002 began this plan in earnest, as the higher energies were about to begin bombarding the planet and we needed to be in our places and ready. With this high concentration of light in the form of lightworkers in certain geographical areas then, there were enough of us in certain places to embody these waves of light as they arrived on the planet.

What began to occur during this time was a shifting or flipping of consciousness and energy through a mass tipping of the scales so to speak, all due to the higher concentrations of light in these specific areas.

Once this was achieved, the energies began to permeate outward to the rest of the planet. The plan worked beautifully, and thus, the Shift Of The Ages had begun in great momentum.

(A brief note: When we finally reached critical mass in August of 2005, lightworkers pulled out their energies of "holding the space" of light, as this purpose was no longer necessary. While holding the space in certain geographical areas up until then, many natural disasters were averted. After lightworkers pulled out their energies, a new energetic space was created where everything was now allowed to fall where it may.)

In the New World, geographical areas are serving a different purpose. As the vibration of the planet has shifted to a great degree, areas that held higher vibrations are basically only matching the overall vibration of the planet now.

Sedona, Arizona, for instance, may appear to be diminishing in vibration, but what is actually occurring is that the rest of the planet has risen up in vibration and is beginning to match what Sedona has always possessed.

There are beginning and will continue to arise, very New areas on the planet that will embody higher vibrations and stand out as the New spiritual centers and hubs.

Southern California in the United States and Hawaii emerged as a few of the first of these locations. The first of the New energies are arriving from under the oceans and through the water (through cleansing and also through the sea with this salt water of our tears and the oceans), and the original blueprint of the planet is beginning to be restored through the Lemurian energy that is being unveiled there.

Eons ago, many of us were the original creators of this beautiful planet Earth. As we have the ability to infuse our energies into many different places, we became, then, the creators of this planet through a variety of forms. And know that in addition, many can infuse their energies into the same form for the purpose of experiencing. For instance, many of us could have been the Elohim, all at the same time. Just as many of us could have infused our energy into Abraham Lincoln and experienced and contributed to being him, all at the same time. If you have an overwhelming love for nature and the planet herself, and feel the most at home while communing with her, I would suggest to you that you were perhaps involved with the plans and expression for her birth into form.

And there are those as well that carry the energy of "tree," for example. They have literally infused their energy emanating from the tree soul family, into a human form in order to assist with this integration and Shift Of The Ages by carrying the tree energy and blueprint in order to teach it to the New inhabitants of the New Earth and to blend in perfect harmony and representation.

I know it may sound strange, but back when I was giving soul readings, there were some who were literally parts of nature and of the Earth herself who were now in human form to relay their special vibration to all on the planet as teachers and representatives of these forms. They carried and embodied these blueprints so well...it was incredible to see, and what a gift of knowledge and integration for us to experience.

As some of us held the blueprint for the original planet Earth within our vibrations, we buried it and its secrets in places on the Earth eons ago, as we knew that it would not be safe for this knowledge and creation to be available for all during the times to come.

So now the New World is being unveiled. It is time for us to usher in this original plan once again and reveal it for all to follow as a perfectly designed blueprint. With enough of the cleansing, purifying and purging having taken place within us and without, it is now safe. Do you remember the plan? Do you remember keeping this blueprint safe in a place on the Earth that nothing would have access to? Do you remember planning to infuse your energy into a physical form so that you could experience these monumental times and be a part of our plan in a physical body, there-by having the experience of feelings and emotions and the whole gamut?

But there is more, and this is the part where your soul purpose really comes into play. The original blueprint for the planet Earth involves the basic plan of energy and creation that originated from the very beginning and all revolves around it. (And know as well, that we are creating a New Earth, and can create whatever we choose, going beyond the Lemurian energies themselves.)

So what is the basic plan? There is a hub of energy that everything shares and that everything has in common. Surrounding this hub are individual and unique expressions of energy that are all different, yet serve to support the shared vibration of the hub as they contribute to its creation. This manifests in all forms of creation. For example, as mentioned in earlier modules of this book, we began as sparks of light splitting off from the Source (or God) in order to experience and express ourselves.

We still share the original energy of the hub (or God), but support it and are connected to it while we express the unique vibrations of our souls.

How does this blueprint apply to geographical areas? Each of the New areas that are emerging on the planet carry a unique and specific vibration or purpose. Although all are connected to Source, they are also unique among themselves.

Each hub or center will vibrate a purpose that supports the overall purpose of the Earth (and that always supports the purpose of God or Source). The higher purpose of the planet Earth is a place to experience, create and expand. Each geographical area or hub will support that purpose, as well.

For instance, one hub (or geographical area) might carry the vibration and purpose of connecting to other star beings and systems and sharing knowledge and visitation. The center or core of that particular hub will vibrate this theme with the greatest intensity and connection to Source at the hub, while each individual residing there would contribute their own unique vibration to that purpose.

The compilation and combination of all your unique and special traits and gifts would carry a common underlying vibration that connects to this hub of purpose, and you would connect and contribute to it in a way like no other. Like an individual and unique fingerprint, your contribution would be vital to the whole and unique only to you. *This space is waiting for you to fill and only you can fill it.*

This basic blueprint carries over to your own unique vibration as well, as you will be creating and expressing yourself in individual modules with many separate pieces that when brought together, make up a total and complete creation and contribution. All the modules and pieces are very valuable on their own, but even more powerful when combined together.

This book you are currently reading, for example, is comprised of unique and individual modules woven together by the vibration of "soul purpose" (as that is my vibration and purpose!). All coming together to activate "soul purpose" within each of you.

Geographical areas naturally vibrate certain purposes in all ways. If you are here with a star connection purpose, your area might naturally have big open and spacious areas that reveal large amounts of sky. Your area might be at a higher elevation, closer to the stars. And there may even be old 3D manifestations of astronomical observatories. You might also be a "night" person as well, coming alive and creating and moving about more in the latter part of day hours and in the evening.

But as most of us know, when we arrive at our own special geographical destination in the New World, it will simply just feel incredibly good and oh so much like home. With no rational explanation needed, we will know we are at our FINAL geographical resting spot on the Earth, and intuitively feel like we are here to stay...it quite genuinely feels like coming back home again. You will know.

And this time, we will be residing in geographical locations that perfectly match our own vibrations and purpose. What a perfect fit and glorious feeling we will have of home on Earth...

Now that the foundation has been laid, it is time to find out more about what you came for.........*YOU.*

As you proceed to the next pages, be ready to connect and activate within you your own special geographical destination of home on the New Earth.

Your Remembering Journal

• • •

Module 7:
Your Geographical Home On Earth

The following pages contain photographs of various geographical spots on Earth. In the spaces below, describe the geographical scenes that you resonated with the most.

_____

_____

_____

_____

_____

_____

_____

_____

_____

_____

_____

_____

- Do you know where this place or these places might be?
- Do you have a sense of what you might do and be there?
- What is it about this place/places that makes you come alive?

Describe what it is about this place/places that you love. Know that you are describing your own essence as well. For instance, a mountainous area with green pine trees might be serene and the desert or southwestern United States might feel "deep and ancient" for you. *These are traits that you embody as well.*

_____

_____

_____

_____

_____

_____

_____

_____

_____

_____

When we finally arrive at our geographical home on Earth, it triggers within us our final purpose. When we finally arrive in the area that totally matches our own energy, we will begin to create our purpose and move forward with rapid speed as the doors literally fly open with this now perfect alignment. This was all planned from the beginning and it is no accident that we end up in these geographical final destinations.

And we do not arrive there until we are finally ready, all in a perfect culmination for our pre-planned purpose to unfold.

You love and resonate with these areas because you are *supposed* to be residing there. And there need not be a specific "reason" we want to be there. These places simply *FEEL GREAT* for us because this is *WHO* we are. Welcome to your new home on the New Planet Earth!

Module 8

•••

Your Bloodlines

*"A water bearer in India had two large pots,
each hung on either end of a pole
which he carried across his neck. One of the pots had
a crack in it, and while the other pot
was perfect and always delivered a full portion of
water at the end of the long walk
from the stream to the master's house, the cracked
pot arrived only half full.
For a full two years this went on daily, with the
bearer delivering only one and a half
pots full of water to his master's house. The perfect
pot was proud of its accomplishments,
but the cracked pot was miserable, ashamed that it
was able to accomplish only half of
what it had been made to do. After two years of
what it perceived to be a bitter failure,
the cracked pot spoke to the water bearer one day
by the stream.
"I am ashamed of myself, and I want to apologize to
you." "Why? What are you ashamed of?"
asked the bearer. "I have been able, for these past
two years, to deliver only half my load
because this crack in my side causes water to leak
out all the way back to your master's house.
Because of my flaws, you have to do all of this work,
and you don't get full value from your efforts,"*

the pot said.
The water bearer felt compassion and said, "As we
return to the master's house, I want
you to notice the beautiful flowers along the path."
Indeed, as they went up the hill, the
old cracked pot took notice of the sun warming
many beautiful wild flowers on the side
of the path, and this cheered it some. But at the end
of the trail, it still felt bad because
it had leaked out half its load, and so again it
apologized to the bearer for its failure.
The bearer said to the pot, "Did you notice that there
were flowers only on your side of
the path, but not on the other pot's side? That is
because I have always known about
your crack. Accepting what was given to me,
I planted flower seeds on your side of the path,
and every day while we walk back from the stream,
you've watered them. For two years I
have been able to pick these beautiful flowers to
decorate my master's table. Without you
being just the way you are, he would not have this
beauty to grace his house."

Author Unknown

•••

BEFORE WE INFUSE our energy into human form, we carefully choose the situations and vibrations we will be exposed to that will best support the purpose or "mission" that we intended to accomplish during this particular experience.

Part of the vibrational environment we choose involves our parents or individuals that we will find ourselves being influenced by the most. When we are still only in our mother's womb, we begin to absorb her vibrations as well as the vibrations surrounding us. We are also influenced by the vibrations in the sperm of our father. This is why we may carry the traits and behaviors of our parents, even if we have not been exposed to them much while we were growing up.

The same is true for transplant patients, etc., who now embody the vibrations of a new organ which carries the vibrations of its donor. But as for our parents or significant caregivers, this vibrational influence is much more pronounced and intended to assist in forming our own unique and special personal vibrations.

These parental vibrations affect us in several ways.

I know a man I will call Dean. With his permission I will share his story. Dean was born into poverty and the only child of an abusive father and very caring mother. Dean's father ridiculed him, ignored him, continually told him that he would amount to nothing, and never kept his word where Dean was concerned. Very arrogant and domineering, he ruled the house with an iron fist. Always busy and accomplishing things, he was also very disciplined.

When Dean was 14, his father told him that if he saved up enough money, he could buy a car. Dean worked and saved his money, and when the day arrived to pick out the new car, Dean went to his dad to tell him his great news that the time was finally here. His father only looked at him and said, "I don't know what you are talking about. I am not going to help you find a new car. Leave me alone and get out of here!"

Around that time, Dean's mother began to encourage him to leave their home. Although a very loving and nurturing woman, her energy told him in many ways to "get out," and that he was not wanted there anymore and unwelcome. She began as well to shoo him away whenever he came near her.

"All men dream...but not equally. They who dream
by night in the dusty recesses
of their minds wake in the day to find that it is vanity;
but the dreamers of the day
are dangerous men, for they act their dream with
open eyes, to make it possible."

T.E. Lawrence

"People are not lazy. They simply have impotent
goals—that is,
goals that do not inspire them."

Anthony Robbins

•••

So at the age of 15, Dean left home, began sweeping out pool halls for some change, and thus began a new life supporting himself.

Dean's destiny (birth) number in numerology is an "8." Eights are here to offer their special gifts of manifesting (especially money) and of making things happen. Dean's expression number is a "2." Twos are here to be the diplomat and to create peace and partnership through their non-confrontational energy of love and support.

Has Dean created the life he came to create and has he accomplished what he came to do?

Dean is now a self-made millionaire. He is the close soul friend that I mentioned earlier who helped me through the ascension process with his gifts of financial support. Being born into poverty created the desire and contrast needed to spur him on to create something different.

Through discipline and desire to prove his father wrong, he fulfilled his intentions of becoming an amazing manifester. Through his experience with his father and the car, he also became a man who always kept his word. Dean is one of the people I know who always does what he says he will, is always there when needed and who stays steady and reliable. To this day, even after knowing him for ten years, I still speak to him several times per week.

In addition, Dean has a special gift of being close and of connecting. Although "eights" can at times be domineering and judgmental, Dean balances this with his desire for harmony through his "two" energy.

He strongly desires union and partnership because of his mother (and his father) demonstrating to him the opposite through their rejection.

Shortly after I met Dean, his mother's spirit appeared at the foot of my bed one night and asked me to tell Dean something. She wanted me to tell him that she shooed him off because she wanted to protect him from his father. It was an act of great love on her part. And at soul levels we souls know exactly what we are doing in order to assist the souls we are connected to for their greatest benefit.

This is why we experience so much contrast to what we are wanting on a global level. Our government and many current leaders here in the United States are demonstrating huge amounts of contrast to what we are wanting so that enough individuals will wake up and want to create change. These beautiful souls are supporting our evolution in monumental ways by serving as beacons of embodying what we *DON'T* want in order to create in enough of us a desire to create and manifest what we *DO* want. They are waving great red flags, trying to get enough attention in order to create change and growth.

At soul levels, we are all always going in the same direction and wanting the same things. We dearly love each other and therefore continually offer to those in our arenas the contrast needed to assist them in their growth so that they can become who they came to be and create what they came to create. All is always in divine perfect order, just as the cracked pot demonstrated at the beginning of this module.

When I used to give soul readings, a common theme was for one partner to create a situation by leaving the other partner, usually through an unpleasant experience. These clients were always very distraught about the abandonment and rejection, but what was actually happening was a great act of love. At soul levels, the "abandoner" was most always leaving in order to offer their partner an opportunity to advance and move ahead with their plan. If one partner was lagging behind, they would usually leave the other in order to free them up for a new and better experience. It was a beautiful and loving gift, very similar to Dean's mother.

How else can parental vibrations affect us? Our parents or primary caregivers also offer us their gifts and talents and we embody them as well with the intention at soul levels to bring them up to even higher levels...

Dean's father had the gift of discipline and action, and he passed these on to Dean who used them beautifully to create his money and all his holdings. Without discipline, "eights" do not get very far. It was an important ingredient for Dean's success.

Dean's mother was very loving and nurturing. Dean has always been a caring man who continually takes his friends and clients out to dinner, always making sure that they have enough to eat and are well taken care of. He also focuses this ability on himself and since I have known him, he has always made sure he is nurtured, well-fed, and takes the time out needed for brief rests. He could not have gotten where he has without these abilities and traits he received from his parents.

As he is here to make things happen, Dean is also an amazing inventor. When he couldn't count on his father regarding the situation with his new car, he learned to take things into his own hands. And because he had so little when he was a young boy, he had to create things from what was on hand. Over and over I have seen him solve a dilemma or create something from what appeared to be absolutely nothing. With the mind of an engineer, he can pull things together that he finds in a barn, for instance, and invent a process and piece of unusual equipment that serves a purpose. These are gifts and talents that he will use in the New World as he creates inventions that serve New purposes yet to unfold.

As we embody the special gifts and talents of our parents and caregivers, our intent before birth was to bring them to even higher levels and to apply them to a New and higher way of being.

My daughter, for instance, is here to bridge the races and create harmony and union between all. Since she was a young girl, she has always had a passion for all people and their unique and different ways. As a child she would draw many pictures of different colored hands all connecting in a big beautiful circle.

She is now married to an African-American man and has two young bi-racial children. She loves the culture of her black family and we have all gotten to know each other well. Through this human experience, our two families have united.

But her two children (my grandchildren) are taking this passion and purpose to an even higher level. My granddaughter Amayah is currently five years old. There are many children in this family...cousins and step-children, etc., who are all very close and spend a great amount of time together. Amayah is somewhere in the middle and the only one without a playmate her age. All the other children have a cousin or stepsister or brother their own age to hang out with. In addition, Amayah recently had a new baby brother arrive who is very doted on by her parents. Being the only boy, his father is enamored with him.

So then, Amayah is feeling especially left out. One might feel great pangs of sympathy for her and her situation if they did not know that this had been planned out at soul levels. Before Amayah was born, we checked in on her soul purpose. She is here to bridge the "nations" and all peoples. A combination of two races in her heritage and within her being, I continually see her seated at the head of a roundtable with representatives from areas around the world. With a beautiful turban around her head and her gorgeous brown skin and magical sparkling eyes, along with her feisty temperament and extreme confidence, she brings together the world. *She is bridging the world races, and therefore taking the role of her mother to even higher levels.*

"You are what your deep, driving desire is.
As your desire is, so is your will.
As your will is, so is your deed.
As your deed is, so is your destiny."

Brihadaranyaka Upanishad IV.4.5

•••

In addition, her birth (destiny) number is a "two," which represents peace, harmony, diplomacy and partnership.

(Her new brother's destiny number is also a "two.") And if she had not had the contrast of feeling left out and alone as a child, she may not have been spurred on to create the opposite.

In the New World, things will be different. As part of the ascension process involves the elimination of polarity, we will no longer develop, expand and grow through contrast and what appears to be darkness.

There is not and has never been darkness, so to speak. At higher levels, as described earlier, all always goes in the same direction and seeks to fulfill the same purpose. At soul levels we always know exactly what is going on and support the all if even through our lower vibrational behaviors and imbalances...just like the cracked pot.

In the New World, the veil is lifting very quickly and all is becoming visible at higher levels. We are no longer in a "play" fulfilling roles. In the New World, as well as in more highly evolved cultures on other stars, our purpose is always known and remembered before-hand, and totally supported by all members in our immediate surroundings.

In addition, part of the ascension process involves a re-union and re-uniting with our parents and families from this particular incarnation for perhaps only a brief time, with the specific purpose of integrating and infusing the bloodlines. In the Spring of 2005, I had the unusual and pleasant experience of attending a very spontaneous and synchronistic family re-union with all my relatives from five generations down. At higher levels we are integrating and infusing the gifts, talents and genes needed as part of the ascension process in order to strengthen our talents through our physical familial DNA, which will in turn support the fulfillment of our designated purpose here. These re-unions with our genetic physical families are giving us the opportunity to "restructure" and "recalibrate" the specific energies of our bloodlines so that they can now be used in a higher and purer way.

The next section of your **Remembering Journal** will assist you in unlocking the higher memories within you of why you chose your particular family or significant caregivers.

Your Remembering Journal
• • •

Module 8: *Your Bloodlines*

Begin by answering the following question:

What were your parents or primary caretakers about? (If you didn't have primary caretakers, refer to the individuals that influenced you the most.)

What did each of them stand for? What did they speak about the most? What was their primary message or theme? What were they passionate about? What meaning did their lives have for you?

_____

_____

_____

_____

_____

_____

_____

_____

_____

_____

_____

_____

As we are here to bring these purposes of our parents and caregivers to even higher levels, we therefore embody the combination of the two. We are usually not completely one or the other, but a combination of both in a beautiful harmonious grey, combining the black of one or perhaps the white of the other.

Combining these two themes of your parents, record how they influenced you and infused within you a purpose or way of being that you are now taking to even higher levels of purpose.

_____

_____

_____

_____

_____

_____

_____

_____

_____

_____

_____

_____

See if you can combine the theme of your parents into one sentence. For example, say your father was all about freedom, self-reliance and independence and your mother held deep values of family, support and stability (or total opposites!). Your sentence might read: "*Combining freedom and independence within a group setting of support and caring.*" A perfect model for the New World and perhaps a vibration you need to embody if your role is to bring that model into form!

Now ask yourself this next question:

Was there a contrast that your caretakers showed you that spurred you on to create and be the opposite? If so, what did this contrast inspire you to become or to value?

Was one of your parents highly opinionated and controlling, therefore creating a strong desire in you for self-expression? Was one of your parents a loner creating a life of isolation for you so that you would crave large groups and social unity? Was one of your parents "absent," creating in you a need to connect with and love people?

_____

_____

_____

_____

_____

_____

_____

_____

_____

_____

Continue with the next question:

What life circumstances were you born into that helped to create who you were, either through its contrast or through its gifts?

Were you born into a large family of connecting and caring relatives? Or perhaps a family divided, supporting you in developing your independence and strong survival and leadership skills? Did you grow up in an area where you could easily connect to nature and animals, or perhaps in a city where you grew to love the arts? Were you in a military family, traveling a lot with no opportunity to establish roots, or perhaps born into a family who had lived in the same town for many generations with staid and specific ideas and habits?

_____

_____

_____

_____

_____

_____

_____

_____

_____

_____

_____

What gifts, desires and traits did your circumstances while growing up offer you?

_____

_____

_____

_____

_____

_____

_____

_____

_____

_____

We were born into our bloodlines so that they could support and assist us in creating who we came to be.

Even though we are spinning off and releasing all of our connections, these vibrations of our family in the 3D are very much a part of who we are. And remember, we are being given opportunities to re-connect with our physical families for brief amounts of time in order to re-calibrate, re-structure and bring anew these family purposes into the higher realms and New World in a much more purified form.

Module 9

●●●

Your One Hat

IN THE NEW WORLD, we will each be wearing only one hat. With the blueprint for the New communities revolving around a central hub with a special and unique contribution being made by each resident, each of us then, will have one special and unique contribution to make.

The ascension process greatly supports this blueprint. As we go through the many internal shifts and changes created by this rare and special process, we begin to get very tired. The ascension process in itself wears us out tremendously, but it also has a jewel hidden within its purpose. Through the stretching, changing and releasing we find ourselves experiencing, we find that we have no energy to do much that we found ourselves doing before.

We have lost the desire for and can no longer be the bookkeeper and accountant, the housecleaner, the car washer, the gardener, decorator and perhaps the cook. It seems we no longer have the energy to *do it all.*

In addition, we may find ourselves no longer being able to jump through all the hoops and red tape that are necessary to get from here to there.

What is occurring is a re-wiring and evolution into the New Human. In the New World, each of us will simply be doing and being what we love. We will no longer have to do or be anything that we do not choose to. We can do whatever we want whenever we want. What is left then, after much cleansing and releasing, is the gold nugget of our passion, fully intact while all else has simply left us. And passion is simply an uninterrupted stream of intense Source energy, all going in the same direction with nothing to hold it back. No doubts, insecurities or fears.

In this New World, all will be fulfilled by someone who has a passion and desire and vibration for it. If there has been a piece or function in the world that no one desires to fill and embody, this piece or function will simply cease to exist. The only reality will be one which is made up of passions and passions, joys and joys and connections and connections.

We are tired of doing it all because we are not supposed to. What we do not choose or desire to do, or what seems to now drain us, will simply be fulfilled by someone who loves doing it, or else it will not be needed and necessary in this New World we are creating. In this way, we will always have everything we need provided by someone who loves providing and sharing it with us and our community as we share our joy and passion as well.

Lightworkers or more "conscious" beings in the old world had many gifts and talents. Because we had been around for so long and experienced so much, at times it seemed that we had a large array of gifts, talents and abilities to choose from. And having so much to offer could cause some confusion on what exactly was ours to do and be!

Therefore, there might be a variety of things that might light you up. Many arenas might be familiar to you as you may have been a master at them in many prior life infusions.

But for this particular time of creating the New World, you came with one gift and talent that was bigger and brighter than the others. Although you are capable of many things, this time that is now arriving will support you in contributing one very special thing, or in other words, wearing one very special hat. It is the hat that is left when you find yourself tired of wearing so many. It is the hat that you continually wear and come back to and the hat that fits the best and gives you the most comfort. It is the hat that you *CANNOT* not wear. It always seems to fall out of the closet and land on your head, time after time.

In my current lifetime, for instance, I have continually found myself in situations where I am "setting up" and then I leave. My greatest joys have been in moving into a new house and getting it organized and decorated.

"I pray thee, oh God, that I may be beautiful within."

Socrates

•••

Living in it is not nearly as much fun. If I were to plant a garden, I would enjoy most the aspects of planning and planting, much more than the harvest. In my prior careers, I held positions of "setting up" as well. For awhile I held a position where I introduced within the schools system a severely disabled student.

I worked with staff, students and outside supports to set up a program enabling this student to be fully supported for success through student interaction and volunteering, staff involvement and outside services. When all was complete and self-sustaining, my job was done.

The same theme was present with me as a grantwriter. I would assist and consult with non-profits in order to help them become self-sustaining, so to speak, and then I would be done. Another time I worked for a large food bank where I supported and assisted over 350 soup kitchens and pantries in 17 counties to help them in becoming more efficient and successful, and then I was done. These self-sustaining principles were also very present with me as a parent. And so on and so on.

What is this theme about? We continually vibrate our soul purpose at all levels, whether in the 3D or in the higher realms. In higher dimensions I hold the same position. I can remember creating planets out of gases (and maybe you can too), setting up the interactive systems of ecology, etc., and then being done. I have continually been a soul who also sets up new planets in other ways. I go to a new planet or system, usually with a team, and set it up to enable it to begin experiencing life or set up the system of life there so that all will function in an orderly way, and then I am done. And this is what I am doing now, and then I will be done with this experience and be moving on to a very new universe which I have never experienced before.

So then, as you can see, we are now coming to a point where we are taking our vibrations of soul purpose that we experienced in the 3D to higher levels of expression. And we are also spinning off all other past experiences and infusions of energy to enable us to wear our one hat only.

"To see things in the seed,
that is genius."

Lao-tzu

•••

Your Remembering Journal

● ● ●

Module 9: *Your One Hat*

In the ten spaces below, record your answers to this question, giving ten different answers:

Who Am I?

For example, are you a mother, father, teacher, writer, gardener, animal lover, music lover, traveler, aunt, daughter, son, renter, landlord, driver, dancer, avid reader, employee, employer, mystic, cook, volunteer, pet owner, nature lover, phone talker, seamstress, consultant, painter, walker, and so on.

1.

_____

_____

2.

_____

_____

_____

3.

_____

_____

_____

4.

_____

_____

_____

5.

_____

_____

_____

6.

_____

_____

_____

7.

_____

_____

8.

9.

10.

After you have completed filling in the ten spaces, answer this question below each space:

What "turns you on" about that particular answer?

Now go back and list them below in order of priority. Your most important priority goes at the top.

1.

2.

3.

4.

5.

6.

7.

8.

9.

10.

Are there any themes that you notice?

Are there any items that if you lost them, life would have no meaning for you? What did you discover that you MUST have in your life?

_____

_____

_____

_____

_____

_____

_____

_____

_____

_____

In this next section, answer the following questions:

Imagine sitting in an airport, waiting for your boarding time. As you have some time to kill, you are not particularly involved in anything. You notice a conversation going on nearby. As you listen, you begin sitting upright in your seat and strain to hear every word, as you cannot believe what these individuals are talking about. You can barely contain yourself, as you really want to jump into the conversation, and eventually do. So then,

What was the conversation about?

_____

_____

_____

_____

_____

Now picture yourself entering a bookstore.

What section of the bookstore do you always gravitate to?

_____

_____

_____

What do you always want to know the most about? Why? What do you love about this subject?

_____

_____

_____

_____

_____

This time, picture yourself in a shopping mall that contains every kind of store imaginable. All you could dream of wanting is in each store of its kind.

Which stores would you want to go into the most? Why?

You can choose more than one store, and remember, they are each filled with everything you could want and more of their particular type.

_____

_____

_____

_____

_____

_____

_____

_____

_____

_____

_____

Now, name three jobs that you have had in the past. *If you haven't had three jobs, name three projects you have been involved in. If you can, also name one job and one project that you are CURRENTLY involved in. Then ask yourself the following questions and record your answers on the lines below each job or project:*

1.

_____

_____

_____

_____

2.

_____

_____

_____

_____

3.

_____

_____

_____

_____

4.

_____

_____

_____

_____

What did you like best about each job or project?
Why did you like this?
Why is this important?

And now some final questions:

What do you know the most about?

_____

_____

_____

_____

_____

What brings you pain and what do you passionately complain the most about? (The opposite of this highlights your gift and purpose.) What is the opposite?

_____

_____

_____

_____

What do people continually ask you for your help with?

_____

_____

_____

_____

_____

When and what do you give without expecting anything in return?

_____

_____

_____

_____

_____

What are you doing when you lose track of time?

_____

_____

_____

_____

_____

When do you feel important?

_____

_____

_____

_____

_____

What do you love doing so much, that you would pay for the privilege of doing it?

_____

_____

_____

_____

_____

When are you the best, most natural you?

_____

_____

_____

_____

_____

Again, pull out all the key words or phrases and organize them into groups or categories. You will find that all your "themes" will fit into the categories you have organized. For example, you may end up with four categories, but most of your answers will be *aspects* or *ways to express yourself* within each of the categories.

_____

_____

_____

_____

_____

_____

_____

_____

_____

_____

_____

_____

As the New World involves a total absence of the responsibilities that we have no desire to fulfill, which is why we "deflate" when we are faced with them, we then get to wear our own special "One Hat." What will yours be?

Module 10

•••

Your Numerology

AS AN ENERGY READER and someone who, then, is very interested in vibrations, I discovered numerology several years ago and immediately resonated with it. Numerology is the science of vibrations and goes back even further than recorded history. Pythagoras, one of the most enlightened men in history, was one of the fathers of numerology. Recorded evidence suggests that it was used ten thousand years ago. It was used by the ancient cultures of Greece, China, Rome and Egypt and found in the ancient books of wisdom, such as the Kabala. As each of us has our own vibratory energy, we are able then, to calculate it by the science of numerology. Numerology believes that each individual can look at his/her own vibrations and characteristics by examining the letter vibrations of his/her name at birth and his/her birth date.

When we infused our energy into our physical forms, we chose many different situations and circumstances that would be present in order to support our purpose this time around. And this time around is a unique and one-of-a-kind experience! All vibration carries certain earmarks, so the letters and numbers in our names and representing our birth dates carry their own special and unique vibrations that define who we are and what we are all about. I have found numerology to be especially accurate in indicating and supporting our own personal ways of purpose, expression, creation and the road we intended to journey upon. And as always, the more progress we have made, the more accurate the numerology seems to be. As we continue to balance our energies within, we more closely resonate with our numerology charts. Over balanced and under balanced personal expressions are simply indicators they we are still on the path of ascension and strengthening our connection to Source. So if your numerology does not seem to sound like you, you have either miscalculated the numbers, or you are "too much" of your traits or "not enough" of them. In this way, your numerology chart will supply you with a good roadmap for your intended purpose and path.

Although complex numerology charts exist, for our purposes we will be calculating and examining the four most prevalent and influential numbers in your name and birth date. These are the **Destiny Number** (or birth path), the **Expression Number**, the **Soul Urge Number** and the **Life Purpose Number**.

To begin, you must use the name given to you at birth, or the one listed on your birth certificate. As there are no accidents and at the higher levels your parents were given the name for you that would carry the vibrations to support your purpose, this is the name we will be applying numerology to today. Even though not consciously aware of it, your name givers were very much in alignment with your soul before birth.

You may have been more tuned in than most when you named your children, if you are a parent, and were therefore guided more consciously to the desired name. Whatever the case, your name at birth is precisely the name you were intended to have.

Each letter and number carries a specific vibration and expression and purpose. When I learned numerology, there was no memorization involved for the vibration of the letters and numbers, as they just seemed to jump off the page with their own story as if they were individual entities and beings all their own. For me, it felt as if they were old friends whom I was meeting again after a long time. This is how vibration works. And remember that it is the same scenario when we meet others in the higher realms and they appear as "blobs" of color and vibration. We can just "feel" them and know who they are and what they are about. No mental energy required. And numerology supports the original blueprint format for energy as well. Many letters come together with differing vibrations in order to create a word or date. All these different vibrations are vitally important for the resulting creation of the whole.

Please proceed to your **_Remembering Journal_** to find out how you vibrate!

Your
Remembering Journal

●●●

Module 10:
Your Numerology

In the spaces provided, write in your full name at birth (the name written on your birth certificate). If you were only given a middle initial, simply write that in. If you had no middle name, that is fine too.

_____   _____

_____

Using the chart below, calculate which numbers apply to each corresponding letter of your name. Write the vowel numbers at the top of your name and the consonant numbers below your name. The example below will show you how. When adding your numbers together, remember to reduce all two digit numbers to one digit, except for the numbers eleven and twenty-two in the **Destiny** and **Expression** number sections (these are master numbers and indicate a higher and deeper vibration). Also remember to include *all* the numbers in your birth year (19___), not just the last two.

Calculating Your Own Numbers

1	2	3	4	5	6	7	8	9
A	B	C	D	E	F	G	H	I
J	(K)	L	M	N	O	P	Q	R
S	T	U	(V)	W	X	Y	Z	

"K" and "V" are master numbers (11 and 22), and therefore left unreduced.

The principal vowels are A E I O U. W is a vowel only when united to another vowel and sounded as one...AW, EW, OW.

To illustrate this process, we will use Mahatma Gandhi.

6	1		1		1	1		1			1			9
M	O	H	A	N	D	A	S	K	A	R	A	M	C	H	A	N	D	G	A	N	D	H	I

M O H A N D A S   K A R A M C H A N D   G A N D H I
4   8   5 4   1 11   9   4 3 8   5 4 7   5 4 8

Birth Date: 10 / 2 / 1869

Soul Urge #: Add all the vowels:
6+1=7+1=8+1=9+1=10+1=11+1=12+9= **21**

21 is reduced to **2+1= 3**

Expression #: Add together all the letters in your name:
4+6=10+8=18+1=19+5=24+4=28+1=29+1=30+11=41+
1=42+9=51+1=52+4=56+3=59+8=67+1=68+
5=73+4=77+7=84+1=85+5=90+4=94+8=102+9= **111**

Notice the triple numbers. In this case, we will not reduce triple numbers, just as we do not reduce the double (or master) numbers. Triple numbers indicate an extremely high vibrating human. (For this section, do not reduce a final number of 11 or 22.)

Destiny **#** is the birth date (*remember to include all four digits in the year*):

10 / 2 / 1869 = 1+0=1+2=3+1=4+8=12+6=18+9= **27**

27 is reduced to 2+7= **9**   (*For this section, do not reduce a final number of 11 or 22.*)

Life Purpose **#:** Add together the Expression # and the Destiny #:
3+9= **12**

Reduced to *1+2=* **3**

After you have determined your final numbers for each category, record them below:

*My **Destiny Number** is:* _____

*My **Expression Number** is:* _____

*My **Soul Urge Number** is:* _____

*My **Life Purpose Number** is:* _____

Now look up the accompanying description for each number in the *numerology numbers* section at the back of your ***Remembering Journal*** (each of the four categories has its own numbers) and you will be led to a description of *YOU*. This is the *YOU* that you came to express, the path where you came to support your purpose and expression, and how and what you vibrate as your special contribution to the world. (There are no triple numbers listed here. Triple numbers simply indicate a much higher vibrating individual. Just add them together to get your general description and know that it is very magnified. For instance, 111 would be a 3.)

To sum things up:

Your **Destiny Number** is **where** (the location or path) you came to place your gifts and talents and make your contribution.

Your **Expression Number** is **how** (how you express yourself, how energy flows through you, etc.) you came to make your contribution. Your expression number indicates your very natural gifts and talents and this is the vibration that lifts up those around you. You bring this vibration to all you do.

Your **Soul Urge Number** is what **motivates** you and underlies all your actions and desires. I personally consider this to be one of the most influential numbers in your chart. Your Soul Urge energy comes from very deep within you and has been a part of you for the longest time. It is very close to your heart.

Your **Life Purpose Number** indicates the specific **purpose** of this lifetime. It indicates what you came to accomplish this time around and what your role is in relation to creating the New World and supporting the Shift of the Ages. It will carry over into your incarnation into the New World.

For all your numbers, see if you notice any similarities in the words used to describe the characteristics of your numbers with any words that have come up in past modules.

List any words that pop out for you for each of your four numbers below:

_____

_____

Module 11

●●●

Your Road To Heaven

"When you do things from your soul,
you feel a river moving in you, a joy."

Jalaluddin Rumi

•••

THERE ARE MANY roads to Heaven, and we are most certainly here to bring Heaven to Earth in a way and on a road that brings us great contentment and fills us with excitement and joy. We are all very unique and different beings, but underlying this uniqueness, we share the same common denominators. Just as we all share the same core fears of abandonment, trust and worth, we also share common desires for our memories of Source and our connection to Source.

Deep down we want to go back...we want to be back where we feel we belong. In this strange place called Earth that we find ourselves in, along with these human bodies, we may feel *abandoned* and left here by who knows what. We may feel that this has all been some dreadful mistake and therefore have no *trust* for the process that left us here. In addition, we may be wondering what in the world we have done that was so terrible that caused us to be put here, questioning our own *self-worth*.

With the ascension process continuing to empty us out in so many ways, we are now finding ourselves connecting more and more to Source and our higher selves, or souls. With much of our old ego parts leaving, and with these New and higher vibrations of light continually pouring down upon us, we can connect and fill ourselves up more than ever before with who we really are. When we are connected to our true selves (or Source), these core issues seem to fall away as we find ourselves in Heaven on Earth. And we each have our own particular road to get there.

As this amazing ascension process involves returning to Source in order to begin again on a clean and fresh palette, we can get there in a variety of ways, all according to what we specifically resonate with in areas of desire, interest and methods of connection.

The basic core of our values, then, involves our strong inner desire to return home to Source where we believe things will feel so much better and all will be OK once again. And since our current "assignment" involves bringing Heaven to Earth, we can accomplish this in a way and on a road that suits us and fits us the best, therefore giving us the most possible pleasure.

We did not come here to Earth to suffer. The planet Earth was designed to be a playground for experiencing, creating and expanding. All levels of consciousness can exist outside the body and outside physical form, but in order for consciousness to expand and grow, consciousness must be in form. It is in form that the creating exists and allows for this expansion...and it was designed to be fun!

And as always, creation and experience exist at many different levels. Energy simply exists. The only meaning it has is what we choose to place on it. Ultimately, everything interacts and connects and experiences according to the universal Law of Attraction, no matter what vibrational level it is on. Like energy always attracts like energy in a perfect and beautiful dance, and now more than ever before, due to the fact that we are existing in higher and higher vibrations, these attractions are occurring more rapidly than they ever have.

We as humans, tend to place meaning on energy because we like an explanation and a story and we seem to love the dramas. Very simply, it is just a matter of physics. Energy attracts to itself similar vibrating energy.

I remember having a strange and unsettling experience while going through the most intense part of the ascension process. I experienced a brief period of time when nothing had any meaning. I could not even remember what a trashcan was for! This was part of the process enabling me to clearly see that the only meanings that existed were what *we* (our ego selves) placed on energies (or creations). If you are familiar with *A Course In Miracles*, it is basically saying the same thing. Without any meanings, energy either feels good or feels bad......it's that simple.

If you have ever had the experience of receiving information from an individual who "channels," you can clearly see this phenomenon in action. When human beings receive energy in the form of information, they want to interpret it and give it meaning. As each of us is uniquely different according to who we are and what experiences we may have had, the same information is then interpreted and delivered in a variety of ways. This is why so many channelers out there can give so many different scenarios for the same occurrence and why Archangel Michael, for instance, can sound like several different beings with totally different messages for us. It is all about the human filter that these energies are running through.

I met a gifted psychic once who was very clairaudient. Her background included a career as a linguist.

Therefore, she receives best and "sees" and interprets best through sound. My interests, passions and past endeavors involve personality assessment. I had a prior position with a management consultant firm where I analyzed prospective employee profiles and assessed their compatibility for the position they were applying for. And my educational background is in psychology, and so forth. Therefore, I naturally "vibrate" personality traits and purposes and this is what I always "see" the most easily when I first encounter a person. Who we are influences what we are able to "see" the best and how we are able to "receive" information from Source. But there is yet another piece to this. Anything and everything that exists for us in our realities does so because we imagined it, believed it or simply made it all up. Energy is simply energy and we like to put it into forms that we can relate to and that help us to feel more comfortable. If you have ever been out of a physical body or been to the higher realms, the story of reality becomes very visible. We have just taken energy and put it into a story or into a form in order for something to do. It is just that in higher vibrational realms, we remember and know this easily.

So then, I would be bold enough to suggest to you that when you are communicating with a higher being or spirit guide, you are simply communicating with yourself. You are accessing a higher part of you and putting this energy into a form that you place confidence and respect in and it just makes things more believable and easy. I personally believe that we have collectively made up Archangel Michael, for instance, but it really does not matter as what our experience is, and what makes us feel good and comfortable, is all that truly matters.

You may have heard of Erin Brockovich. The actress Julia Roberts brought her story alive in a movie with the title of her name. Erin Brockovich was an amazing woman who fought for the rights of individuals who had experienced toxic poisoning through what she felt was no fault of their own. Erin Brockovich began her journey as a single mother with no income. Through a passion and intense vibration on her part of bringing those responsible to justice and making them accountable, she won a landmark case resulting in a substantial settlement. Although not an attorney herself, she was given a large sum of money by the law firm she represented, compensating her for her work. She then went on to become very involved with other similar law suits involving toxic poisoning.

"Great dreams contain inexhaustible truths,
and orient us, like runes, toward our futures.
One hesitates to try to explain them;
one wants to dance them,
act them out in living gestures.
The more we put ourselves into a great dream,
the more we get back.
Great dreams are wells that never run dry."

Michael Grosso

•••

She was carrying this vibration very strongly. As like energy always attracts like energy, she bought a beautiful new home with her new high dollar income that she had worked so hard for. Within a short time, she began to become ill and it was found that the walls of her home were filled with toxic mold, resulting in a substantial expenditure on her part to remedy this situation. Does this mean that she was a terrible person and needed to suffer? Was she "learning a lesson?" Absolutely not. It simply meant that she attracted to her what she was vibrating and what she was about.

Energy is simply energy with no right or wrong, good or bad. There are, of course, different levels of energy according to how fast (or high) they vibrate.

At higher levels, the same is also true for experiencing energies. Many of us have had the experience of creating planets and life forms for these planets. With a desire to experience at many levels, we also infused our energies into some of the life forms we created, and became them. While inhabiting these life forms, we were then able to expand even more and to evolve as well. And again, this is why some of us have an unquenchable love, connection and attachment to our beautiful planet Earth, as we were part of her creating energies. And in this way, we can also make change in another way, as all time exists at the same time as it is not really linear, therefore creating opportunities for changing future through past.

There are also many, many vibrational levels and many, many universes. In this universe in which we are currently inhabiting, we have experienced much. We have evolved as far as we can within this current structure of vibration. As the energies and vibrations have gone as far as they can, we are now bringing all back again, releasing and spinning off all our creations and all the places where we have infused our energies. We have gone as far as we can go. We are now, then, poised to create a brand new planet Earth...the place where it all happens...the jewel and gold nugget of the universe that has been here for all to experience.

And after we are done setting up this new and fresh template and palette for all the future creators and experiencers to utilize and enjoy, and after we are done ascending through the human body while we are alive in order to return again to a closer position to Source, we may find ourselves beginning a brand new adventure in a brand new and much higher vibrating universe. And some may choose to stay here, depending upon their evolutionary status, and become angels and non-physical guides for the newly arriving and evolving forms.

Energy can never be destroyed. It only chooses another form and experience. And we won't be lonely either, as many of us are going to a new experience together with our oh so familiar soul groups. If you have found yourself very exhausted lately and having feelings of being "done" and not wanting to do anymore, I would suggest to you that you are perhaps one of the souls who will be departing for this new and exciting journey to a whole new reality in a whole new universe. And then again, you may choose to stay and assist with the creation of the New World or you may choose to simply go "back and forth" from the New World to the stepping stone world in order to assist others at different stages of their ascension journeys.

For those who are very done and choose to leave, what will happen in the next level universe and what does this new higher vibrating universe look like? I have no idea as I can only see as far as I have been. I have not yet traveled to this new place, so I have no memories or experiences of it and it therefore does not yet exist in any place in my consciousness! What an exciting surprise it will be! Within the vibrational hierarchies or dimensions, we can always go lower by slowing our vibration and dropping our density, but we cannot go higher until we have evolved to that point and are vibrating there ourselves. At all levels, this is how we create our realities, by vibrating and "being" what we want to create and where we want to go. Like energies attracting like energies!

What will be your own special road to return to Source? What will match your vibration perfectly and carry you there through your passions and desires and interests? Where will your own particular "meanings" of energy take you?

Please proceed to your *Remembering Journal* where you will access these answers in a more 3D way.

"If we imagine ourselves as being every bit as huge,
deep, mysterious and awe-inspiring as the night sky,
we might begin to appreciate how complicated we are
as individuals,
and how much of who we are is unknown not only to
others but to ourselves."

Thomas Moore

•••

Your Remembering Journal

•••

Module 11:
Your Road To Heaven

On the first line in the spaces provided for you (1 through 4):

Choose and write down four of your current goals and desires.

1.

_____

_____

2.

3.

_____

_____

_____

_____

_____

_____

4.

_____

_____

_____

_____

_____

_____

These are your futures, and know that if you can envision them, it is because you are *supposed* to have them fulfilled.

After each goal that you recorded, ask yourself this question and record your answer on the line below it:

What do I value about this goal?

For the *values* you listed on line two, ask yourself this next question:

What is important about these values?

Answer this question for each of your four values. A higher and more important value will come to mind.

(You may even have already determined this higher value.) Try and condense it into a single phrase.

If you haven't yet arrived at a single word for your values, ask yourself these final questions and record them on the remaining lines:

What will having the highest value do for me? What will it give me?

Again, answer these questions for all your four values. These answers should arrive for you in a single word.

We can never become passionate about something if it conflicts with our values. And our values are reflections of our relationship and memories of being connected to Source. It is how we felt when we were in the flow of Source energy and closer to God. Your goals are your own particular road back to Source. This was your purpose in choosing these goals.

So then, what is your current road to Heaven?

Module 12

●●●

Your Way To Success

"There is no use trying," said Alice,
"one can't believe impossible things."
"I dare say you haven't had much practice,"
said the Queen. "When I was your age,
I always did it for a half hour a day.
Why, sometimes I've believed as many as
six impossible things before breakfast."

Lewis Carroll from Alice in Wonderland

•••

WE ALL KNOW that what we believe becomes our reality. What we are "being," or vibrating is the fastest way I know to bring something to you. Everything is just more of itself. It's not about having strong feelings this way or that way, as strong feelings on both ends of the pendulum are always still the same feelings...we are vibrating these feelings, no matter what direction they are going in. There is no right, wrong, good or bad. Just vibrations that are similar. Mahatma Gandhi was very strongly a man of peace. He died through violence. Individuals who feel strongly about health, for instance, vibrate all aspects of health. One of my favorite women, Dr. Christiane Northrup, is a proponent and very special supporter of women's health. Being her purpose and passion, she vibrates and speaks of women's health issues, their causes and remedies. Consequently, she succumbed to an abdominal tumor herself. Like Erin Brockovich, what we are vibrating and what we are about becomes our reality, no matter what direction it is going in...positively or negatively (even though there really is no positive or negative).

The key then, is to become "neutral." When we arrive at a place where we realize that everything just *"is,"* with no meanings attached and no agendas, and realize that energy is just energy moving and attracting like energy, it is easier to have the peaceful and successful life we have always dreamed of.

The ascension process has been an incredible tool for adjusting our vibrations and putting us in a state of "being." Through the rigorous process we have undertaken of releasing much of our ego selves and adjusting to these higher realms with our physical, emotional, spiritual and mental selves, we find ourselves in a brand new place, and one perfectly suited to begin our soul purpose.

Feeling as though we do not care about much anymore and being melancholy is a direct and perfectly intended result of this process. It brings us to a place of "neutrality" and places us in an in-between space...in a sense, similar to the space between thoughts and the space we may occupy while in meditation.

We needed to spin off all attachments and all that we thought was this way or that way, or in other words, our misperceptions. These misperceptions were all the illusions and everything that we thought was real. Things were really only what we thought they were. We had made it all up. And in addition, the ascension process made us very tired and we did not *want* to do anything! This was in perfection as well, for if we had jumped out too soon and began doing things and being in the way we had always known, we would not have made progress and begun to create the New. And we are now ready to create from a brand New space of much less ego and much more embodiment of God or Source energy, without our misperceptions.

The ascension process put us in a New place of vibrating much more as Source and being much more neutral to all things, therefore enabling us to create and attract to us what we are vibrating, which is simply Source energy and much more of who we really are!

"A star is best seen at night."

Robert Schuller

"An integral being knows without going,
sees without looking,
and accomplishes without doing."

Lao-tzu

•••

There is one sure-fire way to create what you want, and that is simply to "be" it. Not to think it, "try" and be it, discipline yourself into being it, try and heal yourself into being it or take any kind of action to be it. It is much more fun than that and puts you directly in alignment with Source.

And in the higher realms that we are now residing in and with the near instant manifestation time with like energies attracting like energies, it is far easier to create in the following way:

Find out what you love to do and what makes you blissfully happy and be in that space as much as possible.

It's that simple. And I can guarantee you that when you do this, it will automatically put you in the higher realms and everything will absolutely fall into your lap.

One of my passions is writing energy alerts for **What's Up On Planet Earth?** (www.whatsuponplanetearth.com). Three or four years ago, I began writing these messages. For the longest time, I had this information within me and it was just bursting to get out. It seemed to be all I would ever talk about and I needed an outlet (I'm sure I was driving my friends crazy!). So I began writing these messages and sending them to the friends that I knew who had e-mail addresses. There were about 15 of them. The only other thing I did was to take the article that is included in this program (*A View Of The World Soon To Come*) and submit it to a newsletter that I greatly enjoyed which contained articles that I received via e-mail. That was it.

The article was published, the individuals on my e-mail list forwarded my messages to others, and my passion literally took on a life of its own. I eventually developed a website. In lieu of paying for a web designer, I slip-covered and upholstered some of my original web designer's furniture, as this was another of my passions and joys and I was just learning. She had wanted this done and I needed a website designed, so we traded. Passions for passions, with no money exchange. So I was still able to be in my passion and joy.

"Passion sustains mission."

Greg Anderson

"A champion runner doesn't even know he is in a race.
He runs because he loves it."

Anonymous

●●●

"We need to have more of ourselves
to create what we want."

Suze Orman

"When you get to the truth of who you are,
you can change your life."

Oprah Winfrey

•••

During these past few years, the **What's Up On Planet Earth?** readers have grown to many, many thousands, the messages are read all over the world, published in many, many arenas and the web site traffic is substantial. I have received several offers to publish, edit and promote my books, to be guests on various radio programs, to write for various publications, to speak at many events and have connected to many great and exciting opportunities which have just literally landed in my e-mail in-box...all while I was just following and being in my passion. I have never had to go looking for anything. I honestly did not know that a lot of this was going on for quite awhile, as all I was focusing on was writing the messages and feeling exhilarated when it was time to create one and get it out!

And this is the key. When we are in our passion and joy and being *who* we totally are and expressing this through our creations, then that is all that is needed. Writers who write for the pure joy of writing, with no agendas of being published or well known have a greater success. Actors and entertainers who go to auditions for the pure pleasure of having the opportunity to perform, have a much greater chance of getting the part. It all happens when we do not care or have an agenda. It is when we are simply being who we are and doing what we love that places us in a higher vibration and allows all to *COME TO US*.

This is the way of creating in the higher realms...in the New World...in the next dimension. By "being" who we are, by "being" in our joy and passion, putting us in the higher realms. And, as well, by putting out our intention through "feeling" our intention and then by allowing all to come to us. Being (the spiritual), intending (the masculine) and allowing (the feminine) with no effort required. We need not go looking for anything. We need not "try" and make things happen. We need not intentionally set up meetings and call prospects. This goes against the naturally flowing energy and current of Source. It is about standing still in your space of "being"...it is about simply vibrating who you are and what you desire.

And with much of our ego selves out of the way, there is so much on the horizon for us that we, ourselves, could have never imagined. Oprah Winfrey once said that her talk show was something far greater than she could ever have imagined herself. To her, it felt so right that she described it as feeling like breathing. It was not her idea and she even resisted it at first. When we surrender to Source and to our souls and *allow* all to come to us, we can be ever so pleasantly surprised at what can arrive!

If we can trust that by being in a space that continually feels good by being who we are and doing what we love, we will see that Source takes care of all the rest. We need not do what is not ours to do. We need only vibrate and be what is ours to vibrate and be. We need only wear our "One Hat."

The ascension process also accomplished another readiness feat for us. Although many of us had read and learned much relating to the spiritual world, reading and accepting at an intellectual level is simply not the same as "becoming" and "being" (or vibrating). When we *EXPERIENCE* a philosophy or spiritual concept, it then becomes very real for us. We "get it." We understand it much more deeply. As mentioned at the beginning of this book, the ascension process put us in places where we had to experience. We lost friends, family, jobs, homes and so forth, for instance. We experienced health situations, emotional situations and spiritual situations that stretched us far and deep. We had to begin to walk our talk. We had to literally "become" what we knew and believed. And this is how it all works. Through this process, we began to vibrate the higher ways and concepts we had known intellectually. With much of the lower vibrating ways we had previously embodied now gone, we are oh so assuredly "becoming" living and breathing beings of light.

The year 2005 marked the beginning of bringing the New Earth into form and into the physical. This is the year that many of us will be called to bring forth our wisdom and knowledge to the masses, and especially on into 2006. We needed to "be" it first. This was a key phase and component of the ascension process. In this way, when we enter a room or a space, we can influence it greatly and bring it up in vibration simply by our presence alone. This is also why many of the New material coming forth now will contain audio, visual and other modalities for learning, therefore supporting learning through experiencing.

"The hardest battle is to be nobody but yourself
in a world, which is doing its best,
night and day, to make you everybody else."

e.e. cummings

•••

When we are "being" our purpose and passion, our presence and voice and creations carry this vibration as well. It is all a perfectly designed method and purpose that we are now poised to move into. And you will know when you are ready, when you are able to simply teach and express through **you** alone, with no notes, references or bibliographies. You will be "being" it because you have experienced it. (Have you found that you no longer have a desire to "read' or learn? This is part of ascension...)

The biggest roadblocks to creating our success and being who we are, are *negative thinking* and *victim consciousness*.

It is not necessary to go through "de-programming" and healing sessions to get out of this space. All that is required is to be in a space and surround yourself with activities that make you feel great. We can literally go from one dimension to another simply by thinking a higher or lower thought. When I write, I do not care what anyone thinks about my writing. Through the ascension process, I got too tired to care anymore! And then it became a habit and way of being for me. It greatly helps as well, to simply express and create what is inside of you for the joy of doing it, without wondering, caring or trying to figure out what anyone thinks about it. When we create from within, we are naturally going to activate in others a variety of responses. When others respond, they are simply communicating what *they* are all about and what is within them. Our creations are a light that illuminates all, and much can happen. Some will deeply resonate with you and some will not. There is room for all of us and all our creations. As mentioned many times before, we are only about what is within us, therefore creating it on the outside, and like energy always attracts like energy. We are all just making it all up and placing our own special meanings on energy anyway!

Being in our joy and passion and in a space where we feel good naturally places us in the higher dimensions.

I can remember feeling down and feeling darkness while going through parts of ascension (as we are "in" and feeling the denser parts that are leaving us as well as having our outside world vibrating much lower than we are). My salvation was always to become involved in a fabric art and designing project or to write the energy alerts. I was immediately brought up to a higher level and felt much better. I was in my creativity and in my space of being "me" and certainly connecting to who I *really* was.

Here is what we now have going for us that will greatly support our success as powerful creators in bringing forth the New World that we never had before:

- Much, much has occurred energetically that has created a clear road and a fresh New palette for creating here on the New Planet Earth. Much of the "resistance" energy has been removed.
- I have seen for some time now that we will be totally supported in all ways, including financially, for our passions and projects to unfold. The cake had to be ready before it could be taken out of the oven......all conditions need to be met before creation can occur and globally and energetically these conditions are finally being met during and at the conclusion of 2005.
- We are now residing in near immediate manifestation energy of a much higher vibration. Synchronicities are abounding.
- The planet now matches our vibration instead of the other way around. Up until now, we were residing on a planet with a lower vibration that did not match our visions and ideals. We were in the minority.
- Now that the planet is vibrating higher, basically, what was "up" will now be "down" and what was "down" will now be "up." It is our time. We are now the "rulers" of the planet.
- We have tremendous support from off-planet sources...the star beings. They have come to assist in many ways. They are in my space nearly every day now as we are now residing in more similar dimensions.
- Know that they have come and we need only believe that we can see them and interact with them, and this will be so. And also know that WE are the creators of the New Planet Earth and we are in charge. The star beings are only here to assist at our request. Non-solicited interference does not come from a very highly vibrating being. (And it is also always best to strengthen our power by connecting to Source directly and not by relying on the messages of other beings.) WE are helping our star families as well, by becoming the New Human, which involves the joining of the Heart Human and the Galactic Human.
- The New higher vibrating energies have finally reached the

physical levels and it is now finally time to begin creating in the physical all that we have ever known and wanted.

If you do not know where to begin or what to "do," simply begin by doing whatever makes you feel great.

You cannot go wrong. Just start somewhere. When I began to write this book, I did not know how to start or where to begin. I just started with something, and it grew and evolved from there. It took on a life of its own and built upon each piece of creation and eventually everything totally fit together. I basically allowed it to create itself and was open to seeing what evolved.

A pivotal part in using our Soul Purpose to create the New World involves bringing forth the higher ways and creations and ignoring the older, denser energies. If we become involved with going against what we do not want, then we are keeping that alive by giving it energy and allowing it to reside in our consciousness.

We make it real by thinking about it and allowing it to be in our space. What we need to do is to focus on and become all about what we *DO* want. This has always been the way. It keeps us in the higher realms and greatly ensures our success as creators. In the higher dimensions that we are now residing in, the higher creations will be practically invisible to those residing in the lower dimensions, as will we. As we vibrate higher and higher, will we eventually become invisible as we "ascend" into the higher realms? It will begin by us not being noticed, and then go from there.

Yes, the road is clearly open for us to begin creating this beautiful New World, and now that we can begin in earnest, there will then exist a New World in a higher dimension that all others can access and arrive in when they are ready. We will be creating this space and world where we will reside. And as we can always lower our vibrations and go back to the old world when we choose, we can also, then, go back to assist others in raising their vibrations in order to join us. We are the way showers, the creators and the way to the light. Are you ready?

Are you ready to create the New World? Are you ready to make your unique and special contribution through your passion and joy?

"When I dare to be powerful—
to use my strength in the service
of my vision, then it becomes less and less
important whether I am afraid."

Audre Lord

"Nothing would be done at all if man waited
till he could do it so well that no one
could find fault with it."

Cardinal Newman

•••

———————————

"You are a piece of the universe
made alive. Feel important."

Emerson

"No one like you was ever born or ever will be."

Constance Foster

———————————

•••

Your Remembering Journal
● ● ●

Module 12:
Your Way To Success

Our natural and higher state of being is in playing, being, enjoying and feeling joyful. When we are in this space, we are naturally "connected" to Source and can create effortlessly through our intent alone, while we are simply "out of the way." For many years I found it difficult to take the time for myself to simply do nothing except bask and pamper *me*. I usually had to be sick in order to give myself permission to be in this space and not feel guilty.

But Source has other ideas. We are *SUPPOSED* to be in this space. We are *SUPPOSED* to be having fun, basking, pampering ourselves, and doing nothing but what feels absolutely great and feeds our souls. For quite some time now, I have been receiving e-mails that usually state something to the effect that "I know how busy you are, but..." or "Please address this when you get "time," etc. What most people don't know is that I am never busy. And if they ever find this out, many times they will then ask me to become involved in some sort of "saving" and "helping" project. (Saving and over-helping only serve to deny a life form of its natural process as a powerful creator, and perhaps to rob this life form of the experience of contrast that would serve as motivation for a summoning of something different. And with like energies always attracting like energies, things are always in divine and perfect order. From a higher perspective, things are never as bad as we think. We can become quite surprised when we know for *sure* what the higher purpose of things may be. Sometimes we can be meddlers in a soul's pre-planned process! But there are still times when helping (mostly in the form of "supporting") is the right thing to do as well. Generally speaking, supporting yourself in keeping your vibration high, greatly supports keeping the vibration of the planet high.)

I am blessed to have a life where I can do whatever I want whenever I want to. I have no appointments, agendas, timelines or time constraints. When I write, most of the time I walk right out my back door into the forest and spend the day there writing. Several years ago, when I first began to be in this space and someone wanted to make an "appointment," I would look at my empty day-planner (what is a day-planner, anyway?) and remark, "Anytime is great as I have no life." What I failed to see at that time was that I was simply evolving into the New Human.

And now, if I find myself in a place where I am getting busy and having to make appointments, I know that I am "off," or being consumed by the old 3D reality, and quickly remedy the situation. It doesn't feel good or right to be in that space, and our roadmap to the higher realms is *ALWAYS* to follow what feels good. Promoting myself does not remotely feel good either. In the higher realms, we live in the moment.

While we are simply in our joy and having fun, we will naturally and automatically run into the people that we need to connect with, and find that all we need will find its way to us effortlessly. We do not need to make any kind of "effort," have an agenda, "try," and most importantly, we do not need to become responsible for anything or look for solutions.

Try this experiment for one day each week:

1. In the morning, sleep in as late as you want to. Then go out your front door without any kind of plan or agenda for where you are going or what you will be doing. Simply walk or get in your vehicle and see where you end up. Give yourself permission to stop along the way wherever you choose and experience whatever comes your way that brings you delight and makes you feel good.

Many times while I am writing out in nature, I find myself amazed at all that goes on around me. If I am lying on the ground, I can't help but notice all the bugs and creatures that are scurrying in the dirt, experiencing their own reality. They are in another world. And at times, my cat and I will simply sit or lie together outside and just be present, totally in the NOW, just "being". One time several years ago when I was experiencing this way of being, I found myself on a lonely road near my home in Bayfield, Colorado.

As I was driving, a herd of sheep suddenly appeared in front of me, and I had to stop to let them through. I will never forget the experience of hearing their soft hooves on the pavement and feeling them brush by my car with their incredible fleece. I got a free carwash that day! It was so wonderful not having to be anywhere and not being in a space of going anywhere either. And other times I simply go to the Hopi reservation and hang out with them. These are just a few ideas and examples of how this works, but you will find your own way and own formula.

2. If you do not feel like going anywhere for this one day per week, then stay at home and pamper yourself. Buy a light and easy magazine and read it. Take a long bath with aroma therapy oils. Eat whatever you want to whenever you want to. Spend time on a creative project that you have not been able to get to for awhile. Bask out in the sun (the sun carries the higher energy). Lay on the Earth (the Earth also carries the higher energy). Another great thing to do is to go to a spa or get a massage (not a healing massage, but a pleasure massage). If you cannot afford something like this, put out your intent to experience it and it will come for you somehow.

When we give the universe the message that we are here to feel great and pamper ourselves at all times by intentionally being in this space (at first), the universe will always follow our lead. In this way, it will eventually become a way of being for you and the universe will automatically place you in this space, with no intent on your part.

(A brief note: If you are in the phase of the ascension process where you are still exhausted or having health situations and unable to do much of anything, these exercises are especially good for you. And know that your energy and passion will again return as you progress through the ascension process......as will your health! We all have ascension guides who monitor us at all times and this can help us to know that all is always right where it needs to be.)

All the responsibilities are not ours to do. Let the universe do all the work while we are simply "being" and "basking" and playing and having fun!

A lamp must first fill itself with oil,
before it can shine its light.

•••

Module 13

•••

Your Own Special Team

HOW A FLOCK of geese flies is very similar to our group energy of the New World.

"As each goose flaps its wings, it creates an uplift
for the birds that follow. By flying in a "V" formation,
the whole flock adds 71 percent greater flying range than if each
bird flew alone. When a goose falls out of formation,
it suddenly feels the drag and resistance of flying alone.
It quickly moves back into formation to take advantage of the
lifting power of the bird immediately in front of it.
The geese flying in formation honk to encourage those up front to
keep up their speed. When a goose gets sick or wounded,
other geese drop out of formation and follow it down to help and
protect it. If it becomes able to fly again, the group catches up
with the flock or launches out with another formation."

From Waterfowl Magazine, December/January 1991-1992.

• • •

Because we are rapidly moving into the dynamics of group energy now, with no leaders and with shared responsibility, we are also finding that all the answers and insights we desire are totally within us as well.

And what we seemingly cannot find an answer to within ourselves, somehow gets activated when we combine our energies with others.

We have all heard of soul groups or twin flames...those who vibrate very closely to the way that we do. As mentioned earlier in this book, when we were created at the very beginning, we split off as sparks of energy and light from our Creator, the Source. As this original spark that separated began to separate *itself*, our soul groups were then created. Some soul connections are stronger than others, as these are the souls who originated and were created, then, at the same time. As the souls began separating their energy and dividing it and infusing it into new and different realities and vehicles to express itself, more soul groups were then created from this original soul group. But the original soul group resonates the strongest with itself.

This is why when we encounter certain individuals, we feel as though we may have known them forever. And many times, these same individuals are supporting us in so many ways at soul levels, even though we may feel that they have dealt us a difficult hand and are our mortal enemies! We are just playing the game and have been in this drama and "play" in the 3D reality, and could not clearly see the beautiful and loving support for our purpose and expansion that they were offering us.

In the New World and higher realms, this is not the way it is. In the higher realms there is no need for polarity, as everything is clearly and visibly going in the same direction of Source and light and all polarity has been integrated. The veil is no longer there. Much of this is already occurring as we rapidly accelerate into the New World and higher ways of being. In the higher realms, the masks come off. And even though we may at first not recognize each other, as the forms we are inhabiting may not be what we were expecting, we are most certainly coming together as planned before our arrival.

When we encountered individuals in the 3D world who were part of our soul group, we immediately felt a connection. Because of similar blueprints that Source energy was running through within soul sisters and brothers, we were able to connect more easily with each other and most certainly felt much more of a resonance.

And in the 3D world, we possessed limited thinking with limited ego minds. We needed to have a "story" and drama to place energy into so that we could have a frame of reference that was easy for us to wrap our minds around.

So we frequently interacted in romantic relationships with our soul partners, as we were feeling this connection to Source through certain individuals. Or perhaps we felt great love and connection to some of our family members or even our business partners.

During this time of the Shift Of The Ages, many of us are present here on planet Earth as we had a desire and need to experience, represent and be a part of this grand event. Therefore, many of our "oldest" and closest soul family members are here now in the physical. Some are even here who have not inhabited human form for a very long time, or ever, for that matter.

In the 3D world, we were conditioned through limited thinking, ego, and social mores to believe that we should be with just "one" at a time......in the "romantic" sense. When we "died" or made our transition in the old 3D world, we were always reunited with our soul groups in a wonderful and glorious way. We felt united again and much more whole and complete. This is occurring now, but as we are "dying" while we are alive, we get to meet up with our beloved family once again, but this time while still in the physical!

In the higher realms, we possess much less ego and much more of Source energy. As we are rapidly integrating the higher realms now, this is who and what we are becoming. So how does this all relate?

This means that we will be with more than one partner at a time and that we will joyfully all be together again in our original soul groups. The veil is gone. We will rapidly begin to see who we really are at soul levels and begin again to play, laugh, love and create together. We will have multiple partners. No, I am not talking about the 60's free love and group sex. This is a much higher level of being with very little ego and a great love for each other. We get to be together with more of our soul family, and all at once, sharing, respecting and enjoying each other, as we are most nearly, all one.

As many of us have always known, we will also be inhabiting several "soul homes" together. These homes will be dispersed through-out the planet, enabling our soul groups to always have a place of residence wherever they may be while performing their "purposes." Again, allowing for a continual union with our beloved brothers and sisters, just as we have always done at the higher levels and after our transitions through death.

But there is more to this explanation. In the New World we can create whatever we want whenever we want it. The word "need" will become obsolete. You may already be experiencing this, as at times it seems that just what you need arrives for you very rapidly and easily. It may only begin for you by finding everything you need right in front of you at the store without having to look, or perhaps you just meet the right person or stumble upon the right thing while going about your day. This is only the beginning, as eventually we will become used to this way of being and it will become our New reality as we easily and readily become conscious and very intentional co-creators.

In addition, through the ascension process, we are rapidly becoming whole and complete with no need to attract or become involved with another human being to balance us out and bring to us what we are lacking within ourselves. This was the way of the old 3D world. Like energies attracting like energies in a balancing dance of completion.

Part of the ascension process also involves a time when we find ourselves alone and may not feel particularly comfortable about it. Before we are able to be in unity with our soul families, we must first learn to be comfortable being alone, and this "training period" of being alone and facing our discomfort about it can be quite challenging. But once we go through it and find ourselves content being alone, we will be ready for the glorious union that arrives right on its heels.

So then, we will no longer "need" another to fulfill what we are lacking or to support us or to be there for us or to make our lives complete through "need." And being so connected to Source and the all, we will not "need" another because we are afraid of being alone. In the New World we will connect with our soul brothers and sisters for the simple and exhilarating purpose of enjoying their energy and loving who they are. We will adore each other and come alive while in the presence of our soul group members, not wanting to be without each other as we are so "one."

And yet there is another pivotal reason for connecting again with our soul groups in the physical, and this reason goes back to the very beginning. We have always come together with similar and loving energies in order *TO CREATE*. This is a higher, older and more evolved way. Does this mean that we don't get to have sex anymore? Well, it's certainly not for me to say, but I can tell you that sex is a sure fire way to access the higher realms and connect in a divine way through that incredible kundalini energy, and I personally do not feel that I want to be giving it up! (smile) It creates an incredible energetic space and opening for creating as well. Part of the joy and reason we choose to inhabit physical vehicles is for the purpose of *FEELING* and experiencing with all our senses. This is one of the joys and benefits of inhabiting a physical vehicle.

And you will find that your sexual encounters will become more and more an all over body experience, as your unions with your soul partners serve to activate an incredible energy that takes your breath away.

So as we evolve rapidly, the nature of our relationships will evolve as well. Yes, we will have multiple partners and all love and accept each other in a beautiful and divine way, as at some level we all remember being one. And as we come together in this New and evolved way, we will be focusing on creating together as *TEAMS*. And these teams, just like the geese, will revolve around support.

In order to have something to occupy itself with, Source needed to create. Part of the ascension process, then, involves coming together in teams and bringing forth a project. We knew this time was coming for planet Earth. Haven't we always felt that there was something that we came to do, only we just could not remember what it was? If you have come far in the ascension process, you are now at the place of connecting to your "team" and getting ready to bring forth your "project."

Part of our team also involves members from the stars. In the now higher realms, we are very much closer to the star beings in the non-physical, and they are here and ready to become partners with us as they bring us their expertise and knowledge, blending together with our human energies in a beautiful and perfect dance of creation.

Group energy is the way of the New World. There are no "leaders" in the higher realms, as we all contribute equally to the whole. And as we are creating realities by making everything up and believing it to be so, there is no right or wrong. All of the answers and the clarity lie *within* all of us. We are here now to come together in teams of equal representation to bring forth our contributions for the creation of the New World. In addition, the New human does not shoulder all responsibilities. We do not have to do everything ourselves.

In this module, *Your Own Special Team,* there are no interactive exercises in your **Remembering Journal** as we can't force our connection to or the arrival of our own special team. We will attract it and connect with it when we are "being" it and vibrating it...in other words, when the time is right. When you are ready, and when the "temperature" for your aspect and piece of creation is right on the planet, all will come together in perfect synchronicity and divine timing for your project to occur. The dots of your special team will connect, and when they do, it feels glorious! I can assure you, you will want to weep with joy. The members of your own special team have been having experiences and preparing for a while now, in order for all to come together when the time was right. As all time really exists in the present, you have been connecting at higher levels and communicating and working together anyway. So then, a pivotal point will be reached when all your energies culminate in one perfect place and time. You will be brought together so that your energies can combine as they will then be matching each other and meeting, to bring forth your group contribution.

We really came here and we really exist to laugh, love, play and create together. It was all intended to be fun and joyous! As the ascension process eventually brings us back to our original innocence, being childlike and having fun is our natural way of being...let's enjoy it together!

Module 14

●●●

Your Soul Purpose: Putting It All Together

AS YOU COMPLETE the process of excavating who you are and identifying your own special contribution to the world, two themes become prevalent for "putting it all together":

1. Bringing it all to a higher level for your new residency in the higher realms, and

2. Identifying what "tools" or "road" you use to bring you closer to Source and enable you to embody more Source energy.

All of us who choose to stay here will experience this amazing Shift Of The Ages as we gradually and most assuredly drop our density and begin to embody more and more light. Through the ascension process, we become closer and closer to our souls and closer and closer to Source, all in a natural and perfectly designed process. Remember, we are beginning again and becoming a much more pure form of Source, just as we were in the very beginning when we separated from the original Source itself.

Before we are able to access Source through ourselves in a very direct and connected way (as we are *becoming* Source), we naturally use "tools" or crutches to get us there and create this connection for us.

In the Old World, we may have used cards, pendulums, muscle testing, meditation, speaking with guides or any variety of tools to assist us in reaching a higher level of knowledge and connection. These tools were only an aspect of ourselves, but they worked for us because they enabled us to trust and open to a current of energy that we place much more faith in than we place in ourselves. We also use activities, arenas and lifestyles that bring us joy and seem to resonate so closely with who we are in many ways, thus creating a manifestation of our own special vibrations and purpose.

As we become more and more connected to Source in a much more direct way, we slowly begin to leave these tools behind, as we ourselves acknowledge that we are, indeed, Source energy and becoming a purer and purer form more and more each day. You may find yourself losing your desire to read or acquire any more information. This is a sure indication that you are in your ascension process and creating your own individual connection that is just perfect for you. Knowing who we are, where we are from, and what we came to do and be is a glorious feeling indeed!

For this last exercise, you will need to go back to some of the modules and extract certain information that you recorded in order to pull it all together.

Your Remembering Journal

● ● ●

Module 14:
Your Own Unique Vibration and Contribution

My road, outlet and vision for connecting to Source is *(extract this information from Module 4, #1)* :

_____

_____

_____

_____

_____

_____

_____

_____

_____

_____

_____

_____

This outlet and arena brings me to higher vibrations of *(use #1.a. for your answer here)* :

_____

_____

_____

_____

_____

_____

_____

_____

_____

_____

_____

_____

Some of my goals and purposes on the planet are: *(use Module 4, #2.a. here)* :

_____

_____

_____

_____

_____

_____

_____

_____

_____

_____

_____

_____

_____

My desires serve to bring the higher ways of: *(use Module 4, #3 here)* :

_____

_____

_____

_____

_____

_____

_____

_____

_____

_____

_____

_____

_____

My creation of Heaven on Earth would be *(remember, we are ultimately here on Earth to utilize its original blueprint for simply creating and experiencing on this incredible playground called Earth. Please use Module 4, #4 for your answer here)* :

_____

_____

_____

_____

_____

_____

_____

_____

_____

_____

_____

_____

_____

This is an accurate snapshot of who I am *(your sentence from Module 5)* :

_____

_____

_____

_____

_____

_____

_____

_____

_____

_____

_____

_____

Now ask yourself this additional question regarding your sentence above and record your answer: *Why is this so important and necessary?*

_____

_____

_____

_____

_____

_____

_____

_____

_____

_____

_____

_____

My own special road/s to Heaven are *(use Module 6, Part I)* :

_____

_____

_____

_____

_____

_____

_____

_____

_____

_____

_____

_____

_____

Now take your answer/s to a higher level. For instance, if you said sewing for home interiors, a higher level answer might be:

"Raising our vibrations through creating beautiful higher vibrational surroundings. This would be one of my contributions for creating the New Communities...supplying higher vibrational beauty."

If you can, envision this special contribution of yours existing in the New Communities where you are simply doing what you love to do and supplying it to those who greatly love and welcome your love filled and deeply connected creations and expressions of yourself.

With no traffic, overpopulation, pollution, money, etc., and only an incredible pristine environment totally in alignment and harmony with nature, see yourself living in a beautiful self-sustaining home among sparsely placed homes of others. As you walk in peace and harmony with all living things, and as you magically encounter others in the moment, you naturally offer your contribution and receive their contribution as needed. Entertainment and the arts abound, as do wide open channels to the stars and their inhabitants, whom you have grown to know well. How and where would your contribution to the whole fit in?

What is the higher level version of your road to Heaven?

_____

_____

_____

_____

_____

_____

_____

_____

_____

These are my gifts and my essence, or the vehicle that I utilize for presenting my own special purpose *(use the adjectives from Module 6, Part II)*.

_____

_____

_____

_____

_____

_____

_____

_____

_____

_____

_____

_____

This is the highest part of me, or how my soul *really* and *truly* vibrates *(use the adjectives you came up with in Module 7)* :

_____

_____

_____

_____

_____

_____

_____

_____

_____

_____

_____

_____

Part of my purpose and role in creating the New World is *(use your sentence from Module 8)* :

_____

_____

_____

_____

_____

_____

_____

_____

_____

_____

_____

_____

_____

In my life, I MUST HAVE *(use your answer for the first section in Module 9)* :

_____

_____

_____

_____

_____

_____

_____

_____

_____

_____

_____

_____

Now take what you *MUST HAVE* in your life and bring it to a higher level. Ask yourself, "What would this need to look like before it felt *just right* in all ways?" If you can, create a vision of what this would look like in the New World. Go for the top with no limitations in your thinking and imagining. Remember, we are all here to create and experience, as we are all making up our own illusions in this grand movie...so go for it and make up an incredible story and reality!

_____

_____

_____

_____

_____

_____

_____

_____

_____

_____

_____

_____

Using the key words and phrases that you extracted from the remaining questions in Module 9, create a picture from these themes. For instance:

"Communicating knowledge of ascension through soul level writing in a way that is easy for others to understand. Creating beautiful surroundings through sewing functional fabric art. Creating a whole (unity and connection with others) through individual unique contributions."

_____

_____

_____

_____

_____

_____

_____

_____

_____

_____

_____

Can you define a road/s where you travel that puts you in alignment and serves to unify your connection to Source? Example: *writing, sewing*

_____

_____

_____

_____

_____

_____

_____

_____

_____

This is **WHERE** (the path) I put my talents to use for my purpose here on Earth *(use key words from your* **destiny number** *in Module 10 here)*:

_____

_____

_____

_____

_____

_____

_____

_____

_____

_____

_____

_____

_____

This is **HOW** (my special gifts and talents) I bring my purpose to the planet *(use key words from your* **expression number** *here)* :

_____

_____

_____

_____

_____

_____

_____

_____

_____

_____

_____

_____

This is what **MOTIVATES** me and underlies all my actions and desires *(use key words from your **soul urge number** here)* :

_____

_____

_____

_____

_____

_____

_____

_____

This indicates the specific **PURPOSE** of my current lifetime *(use key words from your **life purpose number** here)* :

_____

_____

_____

_____

_____

_____

_____

_____

_____

_____

Take your last eight or so answers from Module 11 and create a sentence. For instance:

"I am here to embody and teach the higher ways of the higher realms, connecting others back to the way it was intended, using harmony with all representations and contributions of life (including the star beings), while bringing completeness and connection in alignment with freedom."

_____

_____

_____

_____

_____

_____

_____

_____

This is part of your purpose as well......

To Sum Things Up

THIS AMAZING ASCENSION process that we now find ourselves in is creating a truly remarkable human being indeed. Many times we may feel that we are going out of our minds and truly losing it.

Thank goodness for that, because we *are* going out of our minds and we *are* losing it. We are losing all the ego parts of ourselves that we developed in order to survive the 3D world. We are losing much of our density and the lower vibrating aspects of ourselves. And we are losing and releasing all of the places and forms where we infused our energy to experience many different scenarios of reality in many different existences.

And yes, we are losing our minds as we are leaving our old ways of coming from thinking, analyzing, and using our mental processes to create and achieve and heal and grow. In the higher realms, we come from our hearts. We connect from our hearts. We find our way through using our feelings and emotions. There are really only two states of feeling and emotion...something either feels good or it feels bad. If we can allow ourselves to navigate from this space, we will always find ourselves going down a path that fits us the best and creates the shortest and easiest road to Heaven and to our souls.

So you see, you are much more powerful than this book. Your heart and your emotions will lead you to your geographical home on Earth. Your heart and your emotions will lead you to your soul team. And your heart and your emotions will lead you to your own special purpose and to an incredible and magical space where you will totally and completely be *YOU*. This book can only serve to validate within you what you already know at the deepest levels. It can only serve as a support for the powers that already lie within you.

This world would not be the same without you in it. Your presence is vitally needed. We are so glad you are here...

Appendix A

Numerology Number Meanings

Your Destiny Number

This is your **Life Path**. It is the central focus of your existence...the basket to put all your eggs in, or the defining road where you will always travel in this incarnation. Your **Life Path** is the natural direction for your life to take. It is your "home," your "bed," and your habitat. It is the place where everything else within you lies or rests. It is the home or place that all your gifts and talents enhance and where they bring their own special and unique flavor. When we follow our "destiny," our life flows much easier. Your destiny number is **what** you came here to do in relation to **WHERE**. It is predominantly where your field of opportunity lies. It is what everything within you weaves through. It is **WHERE** to put your gifts and talents to use. Your **Destiny Number** is the path you have chosen to take and the role you have chosen to play to fulfill your mission. Preplanned before birth, it is what you came to do and to become...your Destiny!

Please proceed to the pages that follow to find your corresponding number. This is the number that you calculated through your numerology chart in the Numerology section (Module 10) of your **Remembering Journal**.

Destiny Number **One**

The key words defining your **Life Path** are: *Individuation. Independence. Attainment. Creativity. Originality. Courage. Ambition. Willpower. Leadership. Pioneering. Activity. Force. Strong Opinions. Determination. Way Shower.*

Your destiny is **LEADERSHIP**, and you will gain this position through your own initiative, independence, and originality of thought or method. Your success will come from your ability to stand on your own two feet. After you are comfortable being independent, you can then proceed to be a leader and creator.

Your **Life Path** will support you through your great inner strength. You possess leadership, with executive and administrative capability. You have strong personal needs and desires which will assist you in staying strong and independent for the path you chose to be on. A #1 **Destiny Number** feels it necessary to follow his/her own convictions, as you are on the path of leadership and you frequently go where no one has gone before. Self-centered, with willpower, courage and a strong will and determination, you also have a tendency for strong opinions. As you refuse limitations, use your creativity, cooperate without losing individuality, lead, control, and direct, you will be well on your way of embodying your destiny. You perform best when you are left to your own devices, as you are here to show the way to others...so that they may feel free to follow through the independence and creativity you have vibrated. You are here to show others the way to the New World. Your vibration and path results in opening doors for others to go through after you have arrived yourself. Determination is your gift, as you have come to forge the trail where none have gone before. With intent focus and "blinders" on for the outside influences, you know what you are doing in a fearless and forthright way as you must be this way to accomplish your purpose of setting a New and different higher vibrating stage for others.

You are destined to bring this energy and way of being to your area of interest.

Destiny Number Two

The key words defining your **Life Path** are: *Peacemaker. Relationships. Cooperation. Diplomacy. Sensitive. Gentle. Conscientious. Sincere. Refined. Perceptive. Shy. Tactful. Patient. Intuitive. Balance. Detail Oriented.*

You were destined by life to play the role of **PEACEMAKER**. Good will toward others is your magic power for success. You are poised to contribute your ability as an organizer and facilitator in group situations.

You are best being the power BEHIND the throne. Your contribution rarely receives full acknowledgement, but your sensitive nature in alignment with the higher vibrations of Source is greatly needed and appreciated. Arbitration is one of your tools of trade. You are an amazing mediator and diplomat, not liking confrontation.

Sensitive to the feelings of others, cooperative, patient and careful, you are willing to do much detail work if necessary. Although you can be persuasive, you show much consideration for others. You make a good friend. At times you can deny yourself if others can thereby benefit. You have the ability to analyze, to be accurate and to be detailed along with the ability to bring people together for a common cause. You somehow find a way to create harmony. Your awareness, diplomatic skills and organizational talents give you the ability to bring off difficult tasks as well. In a sense you bring Heaven to Earth through your sensitive and caring nature, as your sensitivities derive from your connection to Source. You are here to travel the path of peacemaker, diplomat and arbitrator as you bring harmony to all you encounter. Deeply concerned for others, you seek to know that all is well and to make it so. Your role in the New World is in bringing all together in peace and harmony and "bridging" the energies.

You are destined to bring this energy and way of being to your area of interest.

Destiny Number Three

The key words defining your **Life Path** are: *Expression. Joy of Living. Creative. Imagination. Power of Inspiration. Vision. Cheerful and Happy. Optimistic. Talented. Witty. Generous. Uplifting. Communication.*

You have a creative destiny, and are required to be the **OPTIMIST**. You find great joy in expressing yourself.

You can excel in creative work and are very capable at creative self-expression. Warm, friendly and very social, you have a talent with words (the gift of gab). With a creative imagination, you recognize the possibilities. Your creativity is your gift, but you must have continual focus and discipline, as you can easily become scattered with many creative endeavors. You can be a great inspirational force in the world. Many people have lost the joy of living and it is your destiny and mission in life to arouse their imagination and spirit, until their faith in people and in friendship has been rekindled, and they can laugh again. You express beauty, art, and inspiration in your own life. You are here to bring your gifts and talents to your path of creativity, self expression, communication and joy of living. As a gifted communicator, you will communicate through your creations in an uplifting, inspirational and joyful way as you assist in creating the New World. Always involved in a project, you will bring much to the New World as you express the higher ways through what you create and then present to all others. In this way of loving to share your creations, you uplift us all.

You are destined to bring this energy and way of being to your area of interest.

Destiny Number **Four**

The key words defining your **Life Path** are: *Organization. Limitation. Order. Service. Construction. Practical. Grounded. Foundation. Discipline. Harmony. Dependable. Responsible. Serious. Loyal. Methodical.*

You are destined in life to play the role of **MANAGER** and **ORGANIZER**. You are a builder, and it is your mission to make things permanent and lasting. You use the advantage of order and system when accomplishing your work. You know the rewards of service. You will probably be involved in practical, down-to-earth work.

Patient and dependable, you live with the law of limitation as you are here to be in harmony with the limitations, or in other words, in acceptance of them. You can produce order where little existed. Willing to work long and hard, you are patient and detailed. Conscientious, serious, honest, sincere and responsible, you have strong likes and dislikes. With a strong expression of what is right and wrong, you can sometimes be somewhat rigid and stubborn. You have a natural friendliness, combined with a sense of dignity and self-importance. You do better with a hard problem to solve. Born to take responsibility, others will ask you for support and protection. You will build from the ground up. You are here to provide the foundation in physical form for the New World. You are the dependable support that holds it all up as your path is one of structure and groundedness. Holding things steady for the visionaries and dreamers, you provide a vital service that is very needed in these rocky and tumultuous times of great change.

You are destined to bring this energy and way of being to your area of interest.

Destiny Number Five

The key words defining your **Life Path** are: *Constructive FREEDOM. Dynamic. Independent. Versatile. Active. Clever. Enthusiastic. Change. Variety. Adventure. Curiosity. Travel. Unattachment. Movement.*

Your mission in life is to promote **FREEDOM** and **PROGRESS**, and to keep life moving forward. You can do this by letting go of the old, and realizing the new. There is exhilaration for you with the constructive use of freedom. Life is full of exciting opportunities for you and much adventure. You're capable of almost any task and talented in a number of directions. It is best to pick and choose and to seek experiences that will be of benefit. And best not to waste your time or scatter your forces, as so much will be of interest to you.

Versatile and active, you can do almost anything. Always involved in something new, you are clever and a quick thinker. You can be restless and impatient and may have difficulty sticking to a task, but it is only because you love change. Unhappy with routine, you love to travel. You are a delightful and enthusiastic companion...the eternal youth. Keeping things moving, you are a rapid, quick thinker. Charged with imagination, you have a gift with words. Many experiences will come to you in life. With an uncanny ability to motivate others, you may be comfortable in front of an audience. Discipline and focus are the keys to your success. You are here to assist the planet in moving forward by applying your gifts and talents on this path. You vibrate the momentum that brings this forth. Frequently excited by a new endeavor, you will be able to introduce many new opportunities to others, as you will have your hand in many pies. Traveling to and fro, you will bring much to the world. Your purpose is to get the New World rolling through your great enthusiasm and excitement for the New. You will easily convince others to let go of the old as there is much on the horizon as you fearlessly and eagerly go there yourself.

You are destined to bring this energy and way of being to your area of interest.

Destiny Number Six

The key words defining your **Life Path** are: *Truth. Order. Family. Responsibility. Service. Balance. Love. Sympathetic. Kind. Teacher. Generous. Artistic. Emotional. Counselor. Humanitarian. Appreciative. Adjustment. Charity. Beauty. Sweetness.*

SERVICE to the world is your destiny. Your mission in life is to comfort the suffering, weak, and unhappy.

You also have an artistic destiny, and part of your life's work is to beautify the world. Harmony, beauty, and the ideals of love and companionship are incorporated into everything you do. Things spring into beauty at your touch. You have the deep pleasure of handling responsibility. You are born with the innate ability to support others. You destiny is to be willing to give out much in the way of friendship and love, and always be there to help.

An excellent teacher, you are capable of rectifying and balancing situations. With your focus on family, relatives, and friends, you are an idealist with strong ideas of truth and justice. Much of your success in life will come from the kind and helpful things you do for others. You possess great compassion and are a healer and helper to others. Your task in life is to develop the tools necessary to be truly helpful to others, rather than to simply be a sympathetic ear. You must find the balance between help and interference. You try to maintain harmony within the family or group and are often admired. You need to be needed, but it is best not to carry others' burdens. You are here to apply your gifts and talents on the path of service to others as a teacher, healer or humanitarian. Through your compassionate and caring way, you assist others in raising their vibrations as they enter the New World. Much is elevated as you simply enter a room. You naturally vibrate high and others love to be in your presence as you carry the vibration of refined beauty and love. More than most, you carry the energy of the Mother. As you walk your path, all comes alive and feels great love in your presence. Your purpose is in loving, nurturing and supporting what is already here or yet to be created. You most certainly make the world a better place.

You are destined to bring this energy and way of being to your area of interest.

Destiny Number Seven

The key words defining your **Life Path** are: *Spiritual. Silence. Perfection. Analysis. UNDERSTANDING. Wisdom. Different. Introspective. Observation. Mystical. Reserved. Thoughtful. Selective. Inner Magnetism. Searcher. Alone. Hermit. Knowledge.*

You are destined to be one of the **EDUCATORS** of the world, thereby using your insatiable search after knowledge. You have been destined to discover, uncover and understand the mysteries of life, and to delve into the hidden, scientific and occult. You have to have the peace of mind that comes with knowing yourself.

You have a good mind and intuition. Your life is destined to be devoted to analyzing the world about you, and trusting your intuition. You would be best to learn to be comfortable being alone. Your development depends on your ability to find faith and peace WITHIN.

You are often difficult for others to understand, and to get to know. You depend on yourself and may seem afraid to trust others. Preferring to do things your own way, you may not be too adaptable. You would be best to work in areas where you can use your intuition, mind, and spiritual awareness, without stressing material benefits. With a natural ability to relate facts and size up a situation, you would make a good developer, discoverer, inventor and specialist. Knowledge is your power. You often need to be alone, to get close to nature, and to think and read. Loving to investigate the unknown, you prefer to work alone. Your challenge in life is to maintain your independence without feeling isolated and ineffectual. You are here to share your knowledge and wisdom with the planet, as others will seek you out. Apply your gifts and talents to your path of spiritual awareness and intuition, as this is the road for you to travel. You are here to assist the planet in its evolution into the higher realms by sharing your knowledge of the higher ways with others, there-by opening the door and affirming the ways of the New World. At one with all creations, you understand much. With your gift of wisdom and knowledge, you are here to represent and explain to others how things work and what everything is really about. Your deep understanding makes you a friend to all life forms and in turn, all life forms deeply appreciate your understanding.

You are destined to bring this energy and way of being to your area of interest.

Destiny Number Eight

The key words defining your **Life Path** are: *Power. Overseer. Giving and Receiving. Authoritative. Supervisor. Courage. Perseverance. Will. Material Satisfaction. Organization. Ambition. Self-Confidence. Administration. Executive. Dependable. Efficiency.*

Your destiny will be of **POSITION, AUTHORITY, MONEY** and **RECOGNITION**. Your success will come through knowledge of life, financial effort and determination. Your rewards may not always be in money, but in accomplishment. You are destined to know the satisfactions of the material world and the power which comes with its mastery.

You will most likely be involved with practical, down-to earth work, and concerned with material things (in other words, becoming involved in the physical world). Because you are goal oriented, you can be rigid or stubborn. Good at directing and governing affairs, you are also a good judge of people and situations.

One of your main talents and purposes is in getting things done. Your talents should give you authority, recognition, position and power in the social, professional, and business world. You have the capacity to accumulate great wealth, but effort is required. Your challenges in life are to achieve a high degree of detachment, and to understand that power and influence must be used for the benefit of mankind. You are naturally attracted to positions of influence and leadership. You are here to offer your power and position to assist and help humanity. Apply your gifts and talents to this road of position and authority, and you will support the planet in getting where it needs to go.

You are blessed with the ability to make things happen, and will be a great asset to the New World in this regard. Individuals will turn to you when they want to manifest and get things rolling.

You are destined to bring this energy and way of being to your area of interest.

Destiny Number Nine

The key words defining your **Life Path** are: *Unfolding. Universal Love. Selflessness. Humanitarian. Creativity. Idealistic, but Practical. Sensitive. Philanthropic. Compassionate. Romantic. Socially Conscious. Universality. Brotherhood of Man. Group.*

You came into the world to stand for all that is **FINE, PHILANTHROPIC, CHARITABLE** and **BEAUTIFUL.**

Music, art, romance, drama, color, ideality and perfection are your key themes. You are here to know the beauty of giving of yourself for the deep satisfaction of giving without thought of reward or return. You have come to Earth to understand selflessness; giving up ambitions and material possessions of your own for the common good. The difficulty in this path is the lack of return. Your pleasure comes in the giving.

With much interest in others and a deep feeling for mankind, your disposition is compassionate, generous, sympathetic and tolerant. You are impressionable and broadminded and eager to take on the responsibilities of life, but sometimes meet disappointment because you do not find the perfection you seek in others and in yourself. You have a striking personal magnetism and a marvelous power to influence others and to transform situations to the positive. With a broad outlook on life, you are a Jack of all trades. Rarely prejudiced, you tend to evaluate people on the basis of what they can do for the larger cause, as that is what you are about...the larger cause. You are here to support the whole and know that we are all one. Apply your gifts on the road of Universal Love and Humanitarianism, embracing the many, and you will assist in uplifting the planet, making sure that ALL arrive in the higher realms en masse. You have strong arms that outstretch and embrace all, and greatly vibrate the energy of the whole and of the group. With a very deep caring for the Earth and all her inhabitants, you have come to make sure that all is working together in perfect order and harmony. With a great sense of responsibility for getting EVERYONE involved and coming together for the whole, you make sure the world is a better place.

You are destined to bring this energy and way of being to your area of interest.

Destiny Number *Eleven*

The key words in defining your **Life Path** are: A Master Number (therefore carrying a higher vibration). *Spiritual Light Messenger. Master Teacher. Idealist. Illumination. Capable. Impractical. Dreamer. Inspirational. Revelation. Magnetic. Visionary.*

You have an awareness of the spiritual world and the relation of that world to the material world. With a strong connection to the higher realms and higher ways still intact, you have added perceptions, added awareness, and different capabilities of understanding which take much effort to develop. You are here to spread this **ILLUMINATION** for the benefit of others. You may have nervous tension as you vibrate higher than others and therefore have the inner power to influence the masses and to bring light to humanity.

You possess and inordinate amount of energy and intuition, having far more potential than you know. Ideas, thoughts, understanding and insight can come to you without your having to go through a rational thought process. You therefore have a great capacity for invention. You often feel highly self-conscious as you are so sensitive, but your sensitivities are simply an indication of your connection to Source and your higher level of being. Your desire to achieve some great ambition is enormous, as you know that you are here for some higher purpose. Confidence is the key that unlocks your potential as this world may seem strange and overbearing to you. You have an eye for beauty, and a fine sense of balance and rhythm.

Love, peace, harmony, justice and equality are strongly associated with the number eleven. You are here to travel the road of a higher being. Your purpose in being here is to connect others to the higher realms, as you so perfectly and easily embody them yourself. You are the remembering and the doorway for others.

As you personally embody the higher vibration of the higher realms, you support the planet in its evolution by just BEING HERE. Your vibration alone raises us all up. Apply your gifts and talents to this higher way of being, and you will bring all of humanity and the planet up in vibration.

You are destined to bring this energy and way of being to your area of interest.

Destiny Number Twenty-Two

The key words in defining your **Life Path** are: A Master Number (therefore vibrating higher). *The Master Builder. Organization. Construction. Energy. Power. Responsibility. Inspiration. Capable of Anything. Practical. Unorthodox. Charismatic. Form. Order. Vision.*

Your number is the most powerful and potentially the most successful of all the Destiny Numbers. You must learn the ultimate mastery of combining the highest of ideals with the enormous power to achieve the largest of material goals. You have added perceptions, added awareness, different capabilities of understanding PLUS the ability to attain anything and everything in the way of material accomplishment. You are here to focus your large gifts into productive use. You are here to work for the benefit of mankind.

You find your victory in helping others and in working with large undertakings or groups. You desire and need to inspire others to join you in your dream. You are the visionary with your feet on the ground.

Naturally understanding business, politics, and large institutions, you usually gravitate toward improvement and expansion. You need to embody the right use of power. You possess precision, accuracy, analysis, and determination and are here to travel the road of manifesting in form and of power. As you apply your gifts and talents to this path, you uplift the planet by getting things done and creating large, monumental projects that assist all of humanity. You are a powerhouse that is here to create for the masses, at the highest level. Instrumental in creating the New World in form, your power and influence reach far and wide as you easily and deeply connect with the power of Source and many of the higher dimensions. Almost "unworldly", your energy is much more expansive than the energies of most others. Failure for you is not an option nor a common experience.

You are destined to bring this energy and way of being to your area of interest.

Your Expression Number

Your **Expression Number** is your potential and indicates your natural abilities. These are your own natural talents and capabilities, or how you express yourself. They are the tools that you have to work with on your Life Path, and are usually the abilities you use in the type of work you enjoy. These may also be attitudes found when you express your talents. This is a record of what you are like and what you have to depend upon to make your way in the world. This is **HOW** you express yourself naturally (as you did not have to "learn" this vibration). This is the energy that you bring to all that you do...it is your essence and your vehicle for energy movement that makes its way through everything else and is then expressed to the world as a great gift. Your **Expression Number** is what you **ARE** or **HAVE**, or your identity. This is the way you think. When we are using and vibrating our expression number, because it is a direct and natural pipeline to Source and comes so naturally to us, it helps others to evolve and greatly raises the vibration around us. These are our gifts to share with others.

Please proceed to the pages that follow to find your corresponding number. This is the number that you calculated through your numerology chart in the Numerology section (Module 10) of your **Remembering Journal**.

Expression Number One

You possess executive and administrative capabilities. You are a natural leader or promoter. With your original and creative approach, you are good at directing. You prefer working on your own. Ambitious, determined, positive and progressive, you are also self-confident and self reliant. You have much will-power and courage of your convictions. With broad vision, magnetic force, and inspiration, you like to be in charge.

Courageous and daring, you dream of fields as yet unconquered, heights as yet unattained... the true pioneer. You are the leader, instigator and promoter of new plans and enterprises. With strong opinions and viewpoints, you do not censor yourself. You bring new energy forth through your unwavering determination and strength, daring to go where no one has gone before, there-by opening up new horizons for all to follow. With a laser mind and direct approach, you uplift the planet through your courageous efforts and pave the way for us all.

Others who share your Expression Number: Mahatma Gandhi, Albert Einstein

Expression Number Two

You are the peacemaker. You have a great talent for working with others. You possess tact and refinement. With a highly developed intuition, you are a perfect diplomat. You do better working with others than working alone, and better in a partnership role than a leadership role. You seek balance and peace in everything.

Very sensitive, you are gifted at working with others, but easily affected by things. You are a great support person and good at being the power behind the throne. You often do not get the credit and recognition you deserve, but are none-the-less very needed as you vibrate the higher realms of sensitivity and support. A good counselor, you have an inborn talent for psychology and intuition. Skillful at organizing and handling groups, you are a good facilitator, and can be very persuasive. Capable of handling details well, you are also a good listener. Considerate and courteous, you are cooperative, adaptable, gracious and modest. Tactful, diplomatic and friendly, your success depends on your ability to help others get what they want, rather than being too selfish or self-interested. You are here to support and uplift others through your high sensitivity, wonderful listening skills, and gracious manner. Loving harmony, you greatly help in bringing it forth in all that you do, making this planet a much more enjoyable place. Never abrasive, your gentle approach brings peace and harmony to all your endeavors.

Others who share your Expression Number: Ludwig Van Beethoven, Yoko Ono

Expression Number Three

You are optimistic, inspiring, outgoing and expressive. People see you as cheerful, positive and charming.

You have tremendous creativity and possess good communication skills. Writing, speaking, singing, acting and teaching are possible vocations. With a creative imagination, you express a joy of living with optimism and enthusiasm. Friendly, affectionate, and loving, you are also gracious and supportive. Very social and a good conversationalist, you are cheerful, happy, and merry. Capable of providing inspiration for others, you are an up-lifter to the core. Much of your success depends upon the "vision" and creative imagination you add to your undertakings. You are unusually endowed with talent. You have an innate interest in the world around you and are a good conversationalist because you know so much about so many things. You are here to uplift the planet through your gifts of inspiration and positive expression in all things. Here to be a communicator, you spread joy, hope and creativity wherever you go.

Others who share your Expression Number: Malcolm X, Confucius, Robert Frost.

Expression Number Four

You are the bedrock of society, the foundation of any enterprise. You approach things methodically and systematically. You are a builder and doer who turns dreams into reality. A good organizer and manager, you are good at establishing and maintaining order and routine. Your approach is practical and down-to-earth.

Conscientious and dependable, you can work long and hard. Patient with details and requiring accuracy, you are responsible and can easily overcome limitations. Systematic and orderly, serious and sincere, honest and faithful, you are also helpful, patient, persevering and determined. Very practical, you like to feel sure and not take chances. You like to have a plan. You seem to do better when you have a hard problem.

You are here to build the foundation that turns visions into reality. Holding the structure and space for others, you create into form through your steadfast nature, strong and hard work and loyalty and groundedness. You are here to bring order and structure to everything around you in an unwavering and steadfast way.

Others who share your Expression Number: Julius Caesar, Napoleon Bonaparte

Expression Number Five

You are a free spirit. You love change, adventure and excitement. You love your freedom, and you cannot exist without it. When you use your freedom properly, you are able to develop all of your varied talents.

You are capable of doing almost anything...... and doing it well. Good at presenting ideas, you understand how to approach others and to get what is wanted. You enjoy and are successful working with people. Good at sales, entertaining and amusing, and clever with an analytic ability, you are a quick thinker. Enthusiastic, adaptable, progressive, you love change, like to travel, investigate unusual ideas, and are a delightful companion.

Loving adventure, you are dynamic, independent, and versatile. You add pep and speed to whatever you undertake. Without you, the world could grow dull. You are here to move all things forward and to embrace change with zest and enthusiasm when others are afraid. By keeping the energy moving, you assist all in growing and expanding, and make it a pleasant experience through your vibrant personality.

Others who share your Expression Number: Franz Kafka, Mae West, Karl Marx

Expression Number Six

You are a loving and caring individual with a tendency to put the needs of others before those of yourself. A true humanitarian, you are responsible and trustworthy, with a high regard for justice and honesty.

Harmony and beauty are high on your list of priorities. Your love of children has given you the title of "Cosmic Mother" or "Cosmic Father." You are a natural counselor and healer. An idealist, mainly in the areas of marriage, friendships and humanity, you give help and comfort to those in need. You work well in caring for young, sick or old and show concern for the betterment of the community. You have creative and artistic talents, and love beauty, harmony, flowers, music and the comforts of life. Loving, friendly, and appreciative of others, you are sympathetic and kind, generous and understanding, and are often involved in domestic activities and family. Usually open and honest with others, you have high ideals of truth and justice. You have a natural tendency to serve and teach. You naturally share your gifts of love and support for all others, elevating the planet through your high vibration of goodness and beauty. Vibrating the new blueprint for the New World of the feminine energies, you create a web of the New for all to flow through, nurturing and loving all the creations, New and old.

Others who share your Expression Number: Walt Disney, Marcel Marceau

Expression Number Seven

You are gifted with an analytical mind and an insatiable thirst for the answers of life's hidden questions. You possess clarity and persistence in your search for truth. A good researcher, educator, and philosopher, you have a desire for knowledge and truth as that is what drives you. You need time to be by yourself and value your privacy. With a good mind and intuition, you are capable of analyzing, judging, and discriminating.

You make a good specialist or authority in the technical, scientific, religious, or occult arenas. With a spiritual awareness, you may appear different, and may be hard to get to know. A perfectionist, you are logical and rational. You have a natural ability to relate facts and put two and two together. You would make a good discoverer, inventor, or developer. Naturally reserved, you are thoughtful, silent and selective.

You are here to contribute to the planet through your desire for wisdom and as a never-ending seeking of the higher truth. Always wanting to know more, you assist the planet through your studious and researching nature, while ever ready to share your knowledge (where others have not yet gone before) with those who request it. As you understand much more than most, you greatly enhance the planet with your wisdom and knowledge.

Those who share your Expression Number: Michael de Nostradamus, Isaac Newton, James Joyce

Expression Number Eight

You have the power and potential to achieve great things. You enjoy challenges and rivalry. Money and authority are available to you if you are willing to discipline yourself and persevere in the face of the considerable obstacles in your path. You have organizational, managerial and administrative capabilities. Very efficient, you understand how to accumulate, handle and spend money. You are a good judge of character, and use a realistic and practical approach. You are capable of handling large projects or interests. Ambitious and goal oriented, you are energetic, self-confident and dependable. Capable of coaching, supervising and directing, you are good at taking charge of things. All these talents should give you authority, recognition, position and power in the world. You are here to assist the planet by making things happen. Knowing that it can be done, your love for supervising a project and bringing it into form through your power and connections, brings reality to a vision. Your "can do" attitude creates things when others would rather give up.

You bring a vital piece to the planet by sharing your gifts of taking charge and handling much authority.

Others who share your Expression Number: Leonardo Da Vinci, Bette Davis, Groucho Marx, Helen Keller

Expression Number Nine

You are the philanthropic type......the humanitarian, and have a deep feeling for mankind. Your disposition is compassionate, generous, sympathetic and tolerant. You are inspired to make a better world, and are very idealistic. You are the righter of wrongs and deeply desire to transform the world. You have the ability to influence and direct the masses and deep inside you long for the love and approval of the many.

You could succeed in politics, law, protection of the environment, teaching and healing. With an abundance of artistic talent and creativity, you work well with people. With much human understanding, you can give a lot to others. Your idealism can make you disappointed at the lack of perfection in the world. A romantic, you are aware of the feelings of others. Your challenge is to give to others, expecting no return.

You possess a striking personal magnetism. Rarely prejudiced, it is not hard for you to earn respect and admiration from others. You are here to share your natural gift as a philanthropist, as you embrace all of the whole, and see far and wide. Wanting and desiring Universal Love, you are global in your intent, making sure that ALL are taken care of. You are looked up to by many, and revered by all.

Others who share your Expression Number: Walt Whitman, Charles Darwin, Marlene Dietrich

Expression Number Eleven

Yours is the most highly charged **Expression Number** of all. You attract powerful ideas, intuitions, and even psychic information like unpredictable bolts of lightning. You are a bridge between the unconscious and the conscious, and therefore must learn how to control this powerful flow of energy. You have always sensed that you are different. You most likely had a difficult childhood because of your extreme sensitivity, and this could result in hesitancy and vulnerability as an adult. You often inspire by your own example. With a good mind and analytical ability, you are very capable at almost anything, but often you have difficulty focusing your ability because you are vibrating so high. You usually work better outside the business world.

Very idealistic, you are deeply concerned with art, music, and beauty. Your gift with insight and illumination makes you a natural teacher in whatever area you enter. Here to hold an abundance of light, you need an outlet to express your higher knowledge and higher ways of being. As you run more energy than most, you assist the planet by directing this light in whatever arena your Destiny Number guides and supports you in. You very naturally take everything to a higher level, as you are so very connected.

Those who share your Expression Number: Martin Luther King, Jr., Joseph Pulitzer, Lucille Ball

Expression Number Twenty-Two

You are the Master Builder. You possess a unique gift for turning a vision into reality. You dream big. There is no limit to what you are capable of doing and no limit to what you dream of doing. Your number possesses the greatest potential for accomplishment. You are capable of leading in new directions. You have an unorthodox approach to problems, and much unusual perception and awareness. With a practical approach, you are idealistic. With inner strength, you are able to lead others who follow your vision. You may work for the good of all. You are usually politically astute and globally aware and can be a leader, teacher, and guide who can take control and tell others what to do and how to do it. You have the insight to bring visions into form, and in a powerful way. You know it can be done, and with absolutely no doubt.

You know you can accomplish what others cannot, and there-by assist the planet where others have doubt and lack of motivation. Your great and powerful energy and confidence inspires all and accomplishes much.

Those who share your Expression Number: Albert Bradley (General Motors prior Chairman of the Board), Joseph Kennedy

Your Soul Urge Number

Your **Soul Urge** is what you **really want out of life**. It is your inner motivation and your innermost yearning...what you truly desire closest to your heart. Your **Soul Urge** is the general intention behind many of your actions. It dramatically influences the choices you make in life. The nature of your **Soul Urge** never changes. It is a thread that runs through you from a very deep level, a strength that pulls you along and supports your path...never-ending, always there...your connection at the highest level. This is how you express your deepest connection to Source...the connection to your soul. This particular vibration is what pulls you and guides you and motivates you. I believe it to be the deepest guidance of all the numerology categories and one that truly defines your mission or role.

Please proceed to the pages that follow to find your corresponding number. This is the number that you calculated through your numerology chart in the Numerology section (Module 10) of your **Remembering Journal**.

Soul Urge Number One

The key words defining your **Soul Urge** are: *Leader. Way Shower. Determined. Courageous. Individuation. Independence. Attainment. The Pioneer.*

You have an overpowering need to be independent, and to direct your own life according to what you believe. Your dream is to become the leader of whatever field you enter. You have the courage and the confidence to lead others. You rarely look back once you have made a decision. You are keenly insightful, and good at evaluating the abilities of others. Extremely individualistic, and like to project your own unique persona. You dislike anything that limits your freedom and independence. Whenever you commit to something you truly love, you are absolutely tenacious in your ability to endure difficulties and overcome obstacles.

You are highly responsible and hate passing the buck. You possess remarkable willpower and a strong desire to succeed. You are the pioneer and the groundbreaker. You want to create and originate. You tend to want to handle only the main issues, leaving the details to others. You love the foreground and the hot seat of responsibility. You have all the talents to succeed as long as you maintain balance in your life. If you allow others full expression of their thoughts and abilities, you will easily rise to the top of your chosen field and realize your ambitions. For eons of time, you have settled new lands, new planets, new worlds.

Going ahead of all others, you have traveled the universe where others have not gone before. Unwavering and steadfast, you are sure of who you are and what you have come to do.

Positive attributes: Courageous. Independent. Leadership ability. Opinionated and determined. Opens doorways for others to come after them. An individual. Original. Focused.

Soul Urge Number Two

The key words defining your **Soul Urge** are: *Relation. Cooperation. Peacemaker. Sensitive. Diplomat.*

Deep in your heart there is a sincerity, graciousness and consideration for others. You want peace and harmony in all aspects of your life. You want to devote your life to someone or something. Extremely sensitive and emotional, you need friends and society. You appreciate the refinements of life and desire comfort and security. Your sensitivity is actually a symptom of your highly developed intuition, as you are a gentle soul, and shy away from confrontation as long as possible. You experience a battle within when you do not believe you can handle a situation; this may have a paralyzing effect on you. You are extremely diplomatic and tactful. You function best in a supportive role and want to work with others as part of a cooperative team; only rarely do you want to lead. You will work hard to create a harmonious environment.

Cooperative in your thoughts and actions; you love to share with others and to help those who are in need. You have a natural dread of offending, but you would be best to try to overcome this tendency to inner self-consciousness. You function best in a supportive role, guiding the more public person in quiet, unobtrusive, yet essential ways. For eons of time you have come to be the bridge maker. With a strong desire for all to come together and get along, you make sure that all is in harmony and peace. Uniting one and all, you are here to join the energies of all the worlds you inhabit. *Positive attitudes*: Sympathetic, concerned, devoted. Sensitive, diplomatic, tactful. Emotional. Quietly persuasive rather than forceful. Friendly. Gives love and affection. Intuitive. Loves harmony and peace.

Soul Urge Number Three

The key words defining your **Soul Urge** are: *Expression. Joy of Living. Creative. Inspirational. Communicator.*

You love a good time. You are generally happy, friendly, and outgoing. You have a gift for gab. You are very witty, creative, and playful. You inspire and entertain people. There is little that gets you down. You have a gift for self-expression, and you are drawn to the verbal arts. If your creativity is blocked or suppressed, you tend to daydream and fantasize. Your imagination needs a constructive outlet. Your deeply felt emotional life cannot be avoided or suppressed, and you possess the talent to channel these feelings into a highly creative and artistic form. Art and self-expression are your outlets. You need discipline to make full sense of your abilities. Highly creative, you may scatter your energies in many directions. The key to your success is a balance between the creative forces and self-discipline. Inspiration and imagination are your finest characteristics. For eons of time you have come to create and express. You go to worlds and create things from what you find there, bringing yourself great joy in the unending opportunity of expression. There is nothing that you cannot create or make. Through your creative expressions, you are able to communicate in a way that others cannot. Loving to share your creations, you are able, then, to uplift all others and open a door for them to access new realities.

Positive attitudes: Friendly, outgoing, social. Rarely discouraged. Good mental/emotional balance. Intuitive. Often inspirational. Capable of self-expression, either in social situations or in artistic fields. Uplifting. Supportive. Great communicator.

Soul Urge Number Four

The key words defining your **Soul Urge** are: *Limitation. Order. Service.*

You like to live a stable, organized life. You dislike sudden changes. You prefer orderliness in all things. You have a systematic mind that is reflected in everything you do. Good at establishing and maintaining a routine, you are exacting with details and quite thorough. You desire to be dependable, a rock of strength, and an example of discipline for others. You have a great deal of energy and can accomplish a lot. You may carry the discipline and the need for orderliness a bit too far, especially in your family. FLEXIBILITY is your key to harmony and balance in life. For you, structure is more important then freedom, which you tend to interpret as chaos. Honest and unpretentious, you can be very determined and tenacious. You are the bedrock of any enterprise. You have the courage to go into the nitty-gritty of a problem and come up with a solution. You like to apply yourself to your tasks with concentration and good management. You can be very restless and unhappy when life is uncertain and lacking in security and can be rather serious in thought and action. Loyalty, stability, and dependability mean much to you. Your soul urge is for constructive accomplishment. For eons of time, you have come to hold everything together. With a "rock solid" soul, you hold together energies and rarely waver. With little energy of movement, like a platform and foundation, you keep all stable and secure for all creations to exist.

Positive attitudes: Good at organizing, systematizing, managing. Good at establishing routine and order. Logical, thorough, and exacting with details. Responsible and reliable. Honest, sincere, and conscientious. Practical and analytical. Self-disciplined, determined, tenacious.

Soul Urge Number Five

The key words defining your **Soul Urge** are: *Constructive Freedom.* Freedom is essential for your happiness. You love change, new experiences, meeting new people, adventure and travel. Thriving on variety, you are extremely flexible and adaptable. You are curious, have a sharp mind, and a natural ability with words. You are a born communicator. Generally, you can think clearly in a crisis; you have good mental and physical reflexes. Highly enthusiastic, you get excited easily over a new idea or opportunity. Very socially oriented you are rarely dull or boring. You enjoy being involved in several projects at the same time and may have a difficult time finishing tasks. You love sensory pleasures.

Down deep, you long to please everyone. Your soul has come to bring an excitement for life and all experiences.

For eons of time, you have eagerly jumped into new adventures, new endeavors and new experiences at many levels of existence. Like an eager child, your soul loves the opportunities to begin new infusions of experience.

Positive attitudes: Very adaptable and versatile. Natural resourcefulness and enthusiasm. Capable of bringing new excitement to your interests. Progressive approach and strong feelings. Good mind and imagination.

Soul Urge Number Six

The key words defining your **Soul Urge** are: *Balance. Responsibility. Love. Beauty.*

Your attention is directed to helping and caring for those you love. You are exceedingly domestic. You love your home and family, and work hard to make both comfortable and secure. Your desire to help others is so strong that you may find yourself sacrificing your own personal needs for someone else's. You are extremely loyal and rarely let anyone down. You need to feel appreciation for your giving and caring and want to know that you are needed. You are generous and very forgiving. With a natural ability as a counselor and a healer, you are a compassionate and understanding listener. You are especially sensitive to your environment and your deepest intention is to love those around you, and to be loved in return. You envision a beautiful and harmonious life with love as the basis for all social interactions. Your love is returned manifold; people appreciate you and the love you give, and they are willing to go to great lengths to keep you close at hand. You are firm in your ideas of right and wrong, and when your sense of fairness and justice have been violated, you are apt to be frank, or even bluntly outspoken. Your soul longs for beauty, harmony, and companionship. You have high ideals. For eons of time you have come to spread the energy of love and caring. As beauty and sweetness define you, all scramble to be in your presence as you exude the energy of the Mother. Understanding, supporting and loving, you greatly enhance the worlds you come to inhabit.

Positive attributes: Responsible. Open-minded, sympathetic, understanding, generous. Gives much friendship, affection, love. Expresses deep emotional life. Idealistic. Natural ability to serve, help, and teach; capable of sacrifice if necessary. Artistic and creative expression.

Soul Urge Number Seven

The key words defining your **Soul Urge** are*: Analysis. Understanding. Inner Depth. Seeker. Knowledge.*

You are the mystic and very spiritual. You love knowledge, study, and insight. You search beneath the surface of things and want to know the mysteries of life. A natural with analysis and research, you have a theoretical mind. You may be perceived as cool or aloof and may feel somewhat removed and a little different from others. You would love to be a hermit or monk. Your challenge is to trust. A natural teacher and advisor, you need privacy and time spent alone to cultivate life. You have the gift of intuition, which is your greatest guide and friend. You possess wisdom, a deep understanding of life, and refinement. With a sense of perfection, you aim high to strive for the perfect result. For eons of time you have been the "one" who knows all. Knowing what everything is about and the secrets to the universe, you are sought out by those who are traveling on their journeys, missions and paths. You are the friend to all life, to all nature, to all creation, as they know and remember you well. You understand all creations, and can therefore "become" them and communicate with them with greatness of ease. Therefore, in a sense, you are the representative for all of life.

Positive attitudes: Good mind. Analytical approach. Studious, theoretical approach. Technical, scientific, religious, or occult interests. Reserved. Revered. Knowledgeable. Insightful. Intuitive.

Soul Urge Number Eight

The key words defining your **Soul Urge** are: *Material satisfaction, power and authority.*

You desire success in the areas of wealth, power, and material comforts, but for good reason. You have great ambition. You want to get results and do things in a big way. You have the inner stamina and courage to overcome great difficulties. An organizer, you like to direct and supervise undertakings, and would not find happiness in a subordinate position. You have a desire for money and its authority. You may possess latent powers to analyze or do research work in the field of human emotion and feeling. Your success depends upon your understanding of the laws of life and your ability to master your moods and to cooperate with others. Life expects more of you than the average person. All about power, your task in life is to be able to use power in refined and elevated ways. Without a challenge you can lose balance in life. Your soul yearns and knows well how to make things happen. For eons of time, you have integrated yourself with physical realities, as you understand and become involved with the physical very easily. In this way of becoming involved where others may not, and making things happen in your realities, you bring your special energy and purpose to all your experiences of being.

Positive attributes: Executive abilities. Proceed in business-like manner. Confidence, energy and ambition. Analytical mind. Possess good judgment. Have good sense of material values and are good judge of character. Capable of the imagination required for commercial success. Functions well in emergencies. Inspired by crisis or large odds. Self-controlled. Emotions rarely cloud judgments. You can make things happen!

Soul Urge Number Nine

The key words defining your **Soul Urge** are: *Selfless Humanitarian, Global Outreach.*

You want to be of service to the world. Your deepest satisfaction comes from knowing that you have advanced the cause of humanity. You have high ideals and are a perfectionist. Wanting to make the world a better place, you are fascinated by people from all walks of life. You are highly intuitive and a bit naïve, thinking that all people have the same high values as you! You would love to have the resources to immediately relieve the suffering of others. With a good mind and a great deal of wisdom, you make a natural teacher, counselor, or healer. Even though you want to be of service to others, you may crave fame and the approval of the masses. With a high degree of many past experiences in many life infusions, you may be attracted to the arts, and any involvement with the arts would provide you with satisfaction. Dreaming of having a big impact on the world, you have high expectations. One of your most important life lessons is to forgive. And remember, that for a "9," you receive by giving. For eons of time, you have come to dearly love the ALL......as you embrace much in your wide-stretched arms. With a strong level of caring, you have always desired all to be in peace, harmony and right order. As you come to widely influence the worlds you inhabit, you bring all levels together with the influence of your soul.

Positive attributes: Sympathetic, generous, kind. Sensitive nature. Express love, compassion, tolerance. Possess deep, intuitive understanding of life. Possess innate wisdom, good intuition, broad point of view. Often high ideals and an inspirational approach. Often self-sacrificing. Gives freely without being concerned about any return or reward.

Your Life Purpose Number

All other numbers blend with this one as the ultimate purpose of this lifetime. Although very subtle, your **Life Purpose** number serves as an overall guide for every area of your chart. This is what you came to do in this lifetime...your ultimate goal. As your **Soul Urge** carries with you in all lifetimes, your **Life Purpose** is relegated to this particular incarnation. Your **Life Purpose** will usually reveal itself in your later years, when you are more poised to "give back" as you have matured and embodied much of your soul. And during this one-of-a-kind and unusual time of ascension, this number indicates what vibration you chose to bring to the planet during the ascension process in order to fulfill your particular role.

*Please proceed to the pages that follow to find your corresponding number. This is the number that you calculated through your numerology chart in the Numerology section (Module 10) of your **Remembering Journal**.*

Life Purpose Number One

The **Life Purpose** of **Number One** is in providing leadership and in vibrating independence. Your interests will be in original concepts, new places, new situations, and unique ideas. Other aspects of your chart will support you in becoming a strong leader and director of others, as you planned it this way before birth.

Your own strong opinions and convictions will be a powerful force that can be used spiritually to bring illumination and inspiration to mankind. Your desire to maintain your goal and individuality in life is strong.

You are the "way-shower" and lead the way for all others to follow through your original and determined vision. You usually are the one to "go first" and "see" first, and by doing so, open the door for humanity to leap ahead in consciousness and vibration.

Life Purpose Number Two

The **Life Purpose** of **Number Two** is in showing balance, cooperation, and diplomacy. Twos are here to vibrate their high sensitivity and are able to continually see the light of Source in every aspect of God's creation.

Other aspects of your chart will support you in being receptive to the higher forces and bringing many together for the common goal of all humanity. You are here to be a diplomat and to vibrate cooperation.

You are a natural peacemaker and mediator. Your intuition and heightened sensitivities will be your guide. Your natural humility generated through your strong connection to Source is appealing to all. Like an angel from Heaven, you gently glide between all others, bringing them together through your sensitive, cooperative, and diplomatic energy. You are here to bring harmony to the planet.

Life Purpose Number Three

The **Life Purpose** of **Number Three** is in raising the vibration of the planet through creative self-expression.

Threes are here to express their thoughts and feelings through words, music, art or any other creative outlet. You also embody joy and happiness, and others love being around your positive, joyful vibration.

You are here to make the world a better place through your talents with the arts and in this way greatly help to inspire and raise the vibration of the planet, as well as bringing your gift of inspiration and the joy of living back to people.

Life Purpose Number Four

The **Life Purpose** of **Number Four** is to organize, establish order, and bring ideas and plans into concrete form. You are here as a hard worker as you assist others in bringing their dreams into reality through order, systematic structure and routine. As you vibrate hard work, patience, perseverance and steadfast determination, you contribute to the planet by building the foundation for it to stand on. Very practical, you have courageous high standards, honesty, concentration, a sense of values and application. You are here to bring ideas and inspirations into physical form.

Life Purpose Number Five

The **Life Purpose** of **Number Five** is vibrating freedom, change, versatility, resourcefulness, and being an independent spirit. You are here to support all progressive and forward moving activities. Your life will offer you the experience of changes, new ideas, and an inner restlessness to explore all that life has to offer. You continually seek change. With a love of adventure and a need to be progressive, you make an ideal leader for the New World because of your ability to move forward. As you easily stimulate activity, you can bring a new energy to life. You are here to bring progress and new life to all of humanity. Without you, the world would become stagnant and dull. You easily embrace the Shift of the Ages and our evolution into the higher realms as you hold the vibration and open the door for all others.

Life Purpose Number Six

The **Life Purpose** of **Number Six** is in vibrating responsibility and service to mankind. Highly idealistic, you live on a high plane of life. You expect truth, justice and fairness to ALL. You have a love of peace and harmony, and greatly require this to do your best work. You very easily can become the Cosmic Mother or Father, and need to maintain your balance at all times. With a great deal of love for home and the family, this environment greatly supports you in your endeavors of Life Purpose. As you can be very generous and charitable, you must remember to stay in balance with giving and receiving. You are here to serve your fellow man and all of humanity through your high vibration of love, caring and support. You are the embodiment of "The Mother"......the new energy of the feminine, as your energy lays the foundation for the New World.

Life Purpose Number Seven

The **Life Purpose** of **Number Seven** is in vibrating silence and perfection. Reserved, refined, dignified and apart even in a crowd, sevens live their life in their own way. You depend on your soul for guidance and direction, and learn through inner knowledge of soul realization and higher understanding. Quiet and introspective, you are able to solve all situations through quiet meditation, guidance from within, and going to the higher spiritual laws. Very reserved, you are extremely sensitive and need quiet, rest, solitude, peace and reflection of Source energy. You are here to give your gift of knowledge, understanding and wisdom.

Never one to be "out there" in the crowd, many will come to you for higher answers. Your wisdom and knowledge of the higher ways will assist others in understanding the New World, how and why it is unfolding, and in understanding themselves.

Life Purpose Number Eight

The **Life Purpose** of the **Number Eight** is in mastery at all levels and planes of being. Eights strive to maintain a balance between the spiritual and material world. A leader with authority, you must have a purpose and goal in life. You will handle money and business well by keeping balanced using the power and authority that can guide the spiritual energies into creation. You are here to generate power for the many. You are a natural overseer, supervisor, and authoritative individual, with the courage, perseverance and will to accomplish the goal at hand. As a teacher of the race, you are here to use your natural abilities for the good of ALL humanity. You are here to supervise, regulate, and direct the affairs of others (very possibly in the areas of property and land). Research, investigation, counseling and advisory positions put you in your highest space for assisting the planet. You can get things done and make things happen. With incredible strength, you are able to pull things into fruition when others cannot. With a grasp of the New World and the Shift of the Ages, you will make sure that it is supported and manifests into form!

Life Purpose Number Nine

The **Life Purpose** of the **Number Nine** is in philanthropy. Nines are here to give service to humanity and to vibrate the realization that we are all one, raising the planet from personal love to Universal Love. You are here to give selfless service to ALL. As you are the light of humanity, you will be asked to be all things to all people. Kind and compassionate, you will draw people to you. As an idealist, you will learn to be impersonal. With high standards, you rise to great heights with your ability to restore. You can turn nothing into something beautiful by using your ability to reconstruct and rebuild. You are here to improve civilization on a broad, universal scale. You hold vibration well and for ALL others as you maintain your vision for a higher and better world, encompassing a global intent. A powerful being, you think of everyone, as your arms reach out and hold the masses in your high vibration of universal service. You have a strong desire that EVERYONE arrives in the higher realms of the New World, and therefore hold everyone there by your continued service and giving to the whole.

About the Author

Karen Bishop is the creator of *What's Up On Planet Earth?*, a website devoted to the ascension process and life in the higher realms. Recognized as an authority on ascension, Karen has reached thousands of readers worldwide through her weekly energy alerts about human and planetary evolution, along with the latest information about ascension symptoms and our current planetary status, since 2002.

A life-long clairvoyant, multidimensional traveler and communicator, she has also undergone the challenges of the ascension process . Inspired to use her gifts and talents to reach others going through this amazing on-going evolutionary experience, she continues to give the latest information of our ascension process and life in the higher realms through her mini book series and website.

With an educational background in psychology, counseling and law, Karen has served as a facilitator, counselor and teacher, working with county agencies, non-profit agencies, Native American tribes, public school systems and various individuals.

Currently residing in the mountains of Northeastern Arizona, she follows her joy and passion through writing, sewing fabric art for home interiors (now as a hobby), painting, weaving, enjoying her animals and time in nature, and communicating with and experiencing the higher realms. She is currently working on her mini book series *Life In The Higher Realms*.

For more information about Karen and her latest messages and writings about the ascension process and life in the higher realms, please visit her website at: ***www.whatsuponplanetearth.com***. You may contact Karen through her website.

Printed in the United States
127433LV00002B/6/A